I0562982

bent street 1 . '2017'

Australian LGBTIQA+ arts, writing & ideas

Bent Street is an annual publication that gathers essays, fiction, poetry, artwork, reflections, letters, blog posts, interviews, performance writing and rants to bring you 'The Year in Queer'.

Bent Street 1 – '2017' covers same-sex marriage, health and education, the meaning of queer history and progress; as well as presenting the queer imagination as it follows its own lights, digressions, yearnings, and strange associations.

Clouds of Magellan Press | Melbourne

ISBN: (paperback) 9781925283167
ISBN: (ebook) 9781925283174

Bent Street is published annually by Clouds of Magellan Press, Melbourne, www.cloudsofmagellanpress.net

The Team

Editor: Tiffany Jones
Editorial team and support: Ashley Sievwright, Gordon Thompson, Bailey Wall
Logo: Andrew Liu
Design and layout: Gordon Thompson

Cover image: Guy James Whitworth – www.guyjameswhitworth.com
Interior images:

'Three Owls', 'Untold Stories', 'Chasing Unicorns', 'Inspired Insomnia' by April White – artofaprilwhite.com.

'Butterfluck', 'Flowers', 'So Two-Faced', 'Everyone's a Critic', 'Still Dreaming' by Guy James Whitworth – www.guyjameswhitworth.com

'Bent Street' (digitally enhanced photo) by Gordon Thompson.

Headlines and material from *Star Observer* reproduced with kind permission of *Star Observer*.

Distribution

Dennis Jones & Associates
Unit 1/10 Melrich Road, Bayswater Victoria 3153 Australia
www.dennisjones.com.au

Bulldog Books – www.bulldogbooks.com.au

Submissions

We welcome submissions for the 2018 issue at any time up to 1 November 2018. Please send material to cloudsofmagellanpress@gmail.com. For more information, visit cloudsofmagellanpress.net/bent-street.

CONTENTS

Introduction '2017'

TIFFANY JONES

Welcome to *Bent Street*, the space for all Ls, Gs, and BTIQA+s ... and all letters offending the anti-alphabetical. *Bent Street* is a page for rainbow essayists, yarn spinners and queer theorists. It is a canvas for diverse doodlers and alternative artists. It is an ear for wrathful rants and interesting interviews, an eye for raw reflections and a mouth for personal opinions. Apart from creating a 'Bent' space (make of this what we will), we are an annual space – a collection of works started, finished, or toyed with in the year in which we publish. Some pieces are therefore seeds of ideas, others are well grown or have already borne fruit.

So, apart from a spectrum of writing that happened to emerge in 2017, *Bent Street 1* features work from LGBTIQA+ and allied authors on themes arising from this year. Ah, 2017, when we were geopolitical props at the centre of world politics. When our rights were emphasised in calls to action by the United Nations, and yet fiercely debated in legislative campaigns and nasty online arguments. When we protested the politicking around the funding, de-funding and re-funding of The Safe Schools Coalition (a Non-Government Organisation founded in Victoria in 2010 to combat homophobic bullying, which had expanded nationally). When we were inundated with unwelcome details about family members, colleagues, friends and neighbours' answers to the question, 'Should the law be changed to allow same sex couples to marry?' ... which Malcom Turnbull, not us, had asked. It was a year of abusive posters and pamphlets, Trump & Putin memes, fake news and Cessnas skywriting 'Vote No' above our heads.

It was also a year for elation when two thirds of Australia voted 'Yes' to marriage equality and took back some of the narratives of their LGBTIQA+ loved ones from those who would do us harm. *Bent Street* offers a space for these narratives, some of which may bring up upsetting memories or emotions – please contact the following organisations for support:

- QLife: National counselling service for LGBTI people (www.qlife.org.au) – 1800 184 527.
- Cancer Council: Cancer-specific support services (www.cancer.org.au) – 13 11 20.
- Lifeline: Crisis support (www.lifeline.org.au) – 13 11 14.
- BeyondBlue: Mental wellbeing (www.beyondblue.org.au) – 1300 224 636.

Bent Street 1 (re)considers marriage, health and education debates and the meaning of queer history and progress from multiple perspectives: enjoy the twists and turns ...

Tiffany Jones – Editor
1 December 2017

Three Owls

APRIL WHITE

April's artwork is reproduced in the print volume in black and white — for colour versions, see ebook, or visit artofaprilwhite.com

---

April White began her artistic journey while growing up in London, Ontario, Canada. After completing formal studies in Fine Art, specialising in drawing, at York University in Toronto, she worked as a graphic designer for a few years while planning to pursue her dream of a life of art and travel. The following ten years were spent backpacking across the world, experiencing different cultures, exploring new landscapes and recording her observations and experiences with pencils and paint. Travels led to the west and east coasts of Canada, parts of Europe, Southeast Asia and Australia. Now with over five years of full-time studio work at Lennox Street Studios in Newtown, April's art is being recognised with recent art awards in Australia and in collections across Australia and Canada.

Gaycrashers

JOEL CREASEY

EXTRACT FROM *THIRSTY*

So yes, arguably the worst gig of my life was when I was run out of a small country town by thirty angry homophobes. How's that for the best heckle you've ever heard? Just to be clear, I wasn't literally 'run' out, I was chased and then I got into a car and drove away. Running wasn't an option. I'm not a savage – plus I was in the wrong shoes. I was once again on the Melbourne International Comedy Festival Roadshow. This was the 2011 tour. I was twenty and had been on the road for about six weeks. I was feeling pretty good. I was learning that stand-up was a bit like tennis – you've got to be match fit and it's always better if you're wearing all white. After six weeks of touring and gigging every night with the roadshow, or a month of gigs at the Comedy Festival, you feel pretty indestructible on stage. Your timing is more in tune and you can catalogue your material in your head faster.

We had ended up in regional Victoria. We'd done Warrnambool, Aireys Inlet and Bendigo – you know, all of the rock and roll comedy capitals of regional Victoria, and we eventually arrived in the town of Colac.

Aaah, Colac, Colac, Colac . . .

First of all, 'Colac' isn't a particularly enticing name for a town – sounds like a throat infection or an STD. In fact, I'm fairly sure I got a pretty bad case of Colac after sleeping with a closeted engineer at an airport hotel recently. The town is about a two-hour drive west of Melbourne. And it's built on a lake called . . . wait for it... Lake Colac. The lake itself is – sorry to be blunt – a total shithole. I think it's completely fine to call it that because I'm fairly sure the promotional pamphlet at the local visitor centre calls it that too. Well, it was either that or a 'gorgeous tourist attraction great for couples and families'. Look, it was a few years ago, I can't remember everything.

We discovered upon arriving in Colac that we were performing in a cinema, because the theatre in Colac was being renovated. It seemed that everywhere we went on that particular tour we were never playing in the actual theatre because, apparently, most of the old theatres in these country towns have quite severe asbestos problems, which is fun. Gives it a bit of character, right? Plus nothing makes your audience enjoy the thrill of live performance more than the threat of asbestosis! This could be your last laugh guys ... so make it count!

Actually, in Warrnambool we played the local high school and nobody thought to warn us that half the crowd was deaf. When I saw the interpreter on stage I just thought it was a wildly gesticulating woman who'd gotten lost on the way to the bathroom.

Physically finding the exact cinema we were performing at in Colac was quite tricky as there were about six in the complex. I found that out the hard way when I walked in the wrong door and ended up blocking the projector that was showing *Mr Popper's Penguins*. You better believe my CV has me listed as starring in that film. It's technically not lying. I did. It was just in one very specific screening of it.

On this particular leg of the tour I was third in the line-up. In stand-up, third is always considered a pretty prime position. It means you're on after the interval, so the audience have had time to get in the groove, then have a little break and now they're refreshed and ready for you. They're well lubricated, if you will. But you also don't have the pressure of closing the show.

I went on stage and had quite a good gig, although I did accidentally refer to Colac as Warrnambool. As I said. I'd been on the road for about six weeks and it was my total Britney Spears moment. Do you know that Britney Spears famously gets the town she's performing in wrong? Like, nine times out of ten? I remember going to see her Circus tour in Perth, which was a complete atrocity, but I feel like that's what you're paying for when you go to see Britney. No one wants to see lucid, coherent Britney – I want to see 2007-style, broken down, bald, infant behind-the-wheel, fanny-flashing, nutso Britney. Anyway, she walked out on stage and said, 'Hello, Sacramento! How's it going?' And I remember leaping to my feet elated thinking, this is going to be a good night!

My Britney moment didn't go down as well in Colac. But I managed to win them back and it was a very pleasant gig.

_____

'Hey, mate, I think you're really funny . . .' which I thought was nice . . . I was about to say thank you, but before I could, he continued with, 'But I just want to let you know . . . I still hate faggots.'

_____

Every night after the roadshow gigs we'd stand in the foyer and pose for photos and sign merchandise, which I actually quite enjoyed doing. As I'm sure you've ascertained already, I've been practising my autograph since I was old enough to hold a pen. If I ever get to sign a book for you – let me assure you the pleasure is all mine, and don't worry, I'll be carrying a Sharpie. Actually, only very recently at a fan's request I signed someone's arm. Not knowing she would return to my show the following night having had my messy scrawl tattooed forever onto her skin. If I'd known she was going to do that I would have taken a bit more care. The tattoo looked like the signature of a serial killer ... or a doctor. Or a serial killer doctor. Embarrassing.

On that particular tour I was sharing the stage with musical comedy duo Die Roten Punkte, Daniel Townes, Greg Fleet and Anne Edmonds. Greg, Anne and I would normally group together and make each other laugh while we said hello to people and thanked them for coming. The foyer in Colac wasn't huge, but then it wasn't a huge show, probably only a couple of hundred seats. As I was standing there, a young guy in his mid-twenties approached me with his girlfriend. His opening gambit was, 'Hey, mate, I think you're really funny . . .' which I thought was nice (because it is – duh). I was about to say thank you, but before I could, he continued with, 'But I just want to let you know... I still hate faggots.' And with that he turned on his faggot-hating heel and walked out.

I was really thrown by the whole thing – on one hand he was telling me that he thought I was really funny. On the other hand – well, he hated me. Do they cancel each other out? I was as confused as a chameleon on tartan.

I didn't quite know what to make of it. To be honest, I wasn't overly fazed and I kind of shrugged it off. But I do remember Greg and Anne got quite worked up and upset about it, far more than I did. Their reaction was really sweet and endearing. I felt super special and safe having my comedy family around me, knowing they had my back.

I didn't really think much about what happened until I found out the story had been published in the local newspaper, the *Colac Herald* a few days later. Just by the by, I have definitely caught a bad case of *Colac Herald* before. I think that was on a business trip to Spain.

So! As it turned out, a reporter had been standing in line behind the guy who loves my stand-up/hates my sexuality (hot combo) and had heard the whole thing. The reporter then wrote that I'd been abused and put it in the paper. Which is nice, I guess? And it must have become a bit of a talking point in the town, with people trying to work out who the guy was.

Flash forward a few months later and I had completely forgotten about the whole thing, but a community group called DYNAMIC (a local group for young LGBTIQ teens) called and asked if I'd like to go back to Colac and host an anti-homophobia event. I said of course, I'd love to, and also I was thinking of the boxes of T-shirts I had left over from my days as managing director of PsychYAdelic in Grade 12 going mouldy in Mum and Dad's garage that I might finally be able to pawn off. This group would be teaming up with a similar bunch from Warrnambool who were driving up for the day. These groups are so important for LGBTIQ youths to be able to interact and feel safe with other like-minded people, particularly in regional towns where homophobia is rife. I really thought it was a brilliant cause.

I am always impressed by how brave the kids in those groups are to organise and attend events like that in these towns where there really aren't any gay people hanging out, it's just not the norm. It must be so tough and my heart really goes out to them. There were about twenty other gay guys in my year alone at my school. Imagine being the only gay guy in an entire town. Your Grindr options would certainly be limited.

So off I went back to Colac. I decided to make a bit of an afternoon of it, taking Ashleigh along (I needed someone with a car) and our friends Kate and Andy. The drive there was really fun, listening to musical soundtracks and stopping for lunch in Geelong. I know! My life is so glamorous!

Around early afternoon we arrived in Colac for the event. The function was being held in a local bar called Straight Shooters (Christ, the irony, I cannot *begin* to tell you!). I think it was a bar – but who knows? It had a bit of a saloon-type vibe. The actual bar itself wasn't open, so that was a bit of a bummer. I mean what's a trip to Colac without a cocktail, I always say.

There was quite a big turnout there, and I thought, surely all these people can't be the local gay kids? Turns out they weren't. There were also a lot of … what would you call them? Hoodlums, thugs, ruffians? Little fucking shits? They were walking around the event giving the LGBTIQ kids a really hard time. They were easy to spot, too, in their hoodies and Globe shoes, reeking of Lynx Africa and broken homes.

I aired what I had seen with one of the people running the event, but they were a bit snowed under themselves – there were only two organisers, and it was such a tough job, their hands were already full. So I took it upon myself to have a bit of a word with some of these little arseholes. What was going on at that stage wasn't too major and the event was still in full swing, it was just the odd comment made here and there and nobody really standing up for themselves. And look, fair enough. Why would they want to? They probably had to go to school with these bullies.

But I did my bit and MCed the event and it all went well. Besides, by the time I got on stage most of the bullies had left, it seemed. I was there for a couple of hours and then it was time for me and my mates to leave. We had ice-creams to purchase in Geelong! We said goodbye to everyone and left the venue.

Unfortunately, we didn't get the Golden Gaytime we were after.

When we got outside Straight Shooters there were about twenty kids, sixteen or seventeen year olds – basically grown men – waiting on the street to pick a fight. They started yelling at me and my friends, calling us faggots and telling us to burn in hell. We ignored them and kept walking, but they started to really press in on us. It seemed like more and more of them were appearing. In the end there were about thirty of them.

It didn't quite register with me what was happening. It was surreal.

We were keeping our heads down as we tried to walk through them to get to the car, but they started shoving us, and it was really hard not to snap back. Then they started pushing and shouldering us.

Finally Ashleigh, summoning the verbal strength she had exhibited at that schoolyard tennis march of our youth, told one of them to go fuck themselves. I think it's essentially become her catch-phrase.

They didn't take that well. Two seconds later, we were running to Ashleigh's little Holden Astra as a couple of plastic Coke bottles were thrown at us (thank God – imagine if they had glass?). They missed. It's a sad day when a faggot has better aim than you. We jumped in the car and were off. I remember turning around in my seat and seeing these thirty kids yelling homophobic, disgusting abuse at us, every vile thing under the sun. Mostly one-syllable words though, let's be honest.

It's a strange feeling to turn around and see a group of people yelling, 'If you ever come back we'll kill you, faggot!' Like, stop being so obsessed with me. Who has that sort of time?

In all honesty, I was shaking. I cried a bit. But the thing is, I'm Gen Y, I have priorities, so I still found time to tweet about it. And it blew up immediately. It went *crazy*. It was in every paper, all over the news, I had to do radio interviews about it (and you know how I hate attention). It even made international news because my friend saw it in a magazine in Changi Airport in Singapore, which totally counts. It was a big deal. My profile was only on the start of a rise at this point, but it was a big story. A gay entertainer was chased from a town – the irony being he was chased from an anti-homophobia event.

———————————

I'm not sure how they specifically pitched it, but I'm guessing 'Let's put these homos in serious danger' would probably have gotten it across the line.

———————————

I probably should've told my mum. She called me, panicked, having read it in the paper. I took the call during the intermission of *Love Never Dies*, the sequel to *Phantom of the Opera*, and the show was about to start again and I had to quickly explain to her what had happened before hissing, 'Mum, I've got to go, the Phantom is about to come back.' She was even more confused.

The silver lining of the whole incident and something these homophobic cocksnaps didn't realise, was that my exposure went through the roof as a result of that incident and I scored an invite to the *Sex and the City 2* premiere in Sydney, where I totally met Sarah Jessica Parker and told her she had fabulous shoes and she replied, 'Thanks, girlfriend!' and we sassy clicked at each other.

So essentially those homophobes were the direct cause of the gayest thing that had happened to me up to that point. (*Thanks, boys, if you're reading this. Hope you're doing well and you're really happy with all your life choices. PS. Please don't reproduce. Joel x*).

You'd think I was done with Colac at that point, never to return. But at the end of 2013 I went back with one of my best friends, a brilliant comedian called Rhys Nicholson, who is also gay (he says, but apart from being engaged to a man I am yet to see proof) and a film crew to make an anti-homophobia documentary, because after all the press about what had happened to me, Colac had earned the reputation as the most homophobic town in Australia. I actually think it was on

Colac's Wikipedia entry for a while, but some local councillor probably frantically edits it off every time it goes up.

The film crew we went back to Colac with was headed by the brilliant Tom Rohr and Nel Minchin (sister of Tim Minchin and Katie Minchin, my tour manager in that rural town with the radio station). They had won a grant to fund the idea and were filming the doco for ABC2. I'm not sure how they specifically pitched it, but I'm guessing 'Let's put these homos in serious danger' would probably have gotten it across the line.

We had a coffee on camera and it was extremely uncomfortable. She told me that as a result of my actions in the media, the group had lost its funding and had disbanded.

The doco was called *Gaycrashers*. It really is one of the pieces of work I am most proud of and it was amazing to experience it with such a fabulous person as Rhys. We were in Colac filming for a week and Rhys and I did things like working at the local timber mill and the pub. Then at the end of the week we put on a show, having sold tickets on our rounds of the towns businesses. The test being: will the town be comfortable enough to buy a ticket to support and watch two gay comedians?

It was interesting because nobody was really openly homophobic to us on camera but it was also frustrating because people would drive down the street and shout out, 'Faggots!' or 'Homos!', and because it was such a small film crew it was really hard to capture that stuff on camera. It takes a brave person to yell abuse at someone out of a car window and drive off. I'm sure they have *huge* penises and *great* jobs and *really* happy home lives.

Other people we encountered, though, were on their best behaviour after an article appeared in the *Colac Herald* almost instructing locals not to fuck up while the cameras were around. We read that and thought wow, what a way to brush the issue under the carpet. What happens when we're not around?

One of the really shocking things that happened during my time there was that I spoke to Emma, who ran DYNAMIC and had been involved in organising the anti-homophobia event I'd been chased from. We had a coffee on camera and it was extremely uncomfortable. She told me that as a result of my actions in the media, the group had lost its funding and had disbanded. Even worse, she told me it really hadn't been good for the LGBTIQ kids in the town, resulting in further bullying.

It broke my heart that my actions had had a carry-on effect for those kids, because I really didn't want to make their lives any harder than they already were.

When the incident happened and I went to the media I was only twenty, and perhaps it was ignorance on my part, but I truly believed that getting that media attention would help the cause and shine a light on the issue. And perhaps locals would be more vigilant and keep an eye out for any bullying. But instead the locals turned against the anti-homophobia group. They were anti-anti-homophobic, if you will. During the whole media frenzy following the Colac incident, I was taking advice from publicists, from managers, and yes – part of me was trying to look out for my own career. But I truly thought I was championing these kids by being in the spotlight.

In the end, Emma and I had to agree to disagree. I remember leaving the chat with Emma furious. We were on the same page, both fighting homophobia - why on earth would she attack me and bring that up on camera? But now, a few years on, I totally understand what Emma had to say. And I thank Meryl Streep that Colac has someone like Emma looking out for these kids.

But there were some positive changes that had been made between my first and second visits. The mayor who was there when I was first chased out of town had been replaced. This is the same mayor, by the way, who, in an ABC interview to defend his town during the media backlash, said, 'Well, it's not like there were any sticks or bottles thrown or any bones broken!' I think even the town knew this was a bonkers thing to say because he was voted out at the following election and replaced by new mayor Lyn Russell. Rhys and I met with Lyn and she was gorgeous and exactly what the town needed.

The end of the documentary shows our local stand-up night, which we had been selling tickets to over our week in Colac. The show was quite bittersweet: not many people turned up to see us perform, only about thirty, which was really sad. I think more people would have come if the cameras hadn't been there. Perhaps they didn't want to be seen publicly supporting two gay guys.

What was really sweet was that the mayor, Lyn, gave a speech at the start of the show before welcoming Rhys to the stage. It was a really beautiful speech, saying that people should be free to love whoever they like, and nobody should be allowed to get in the way of that. That was really fucking cool and I have so much respect for Lyn for doing that. I think if regional towns had more people like her leading the community, then issues like homophobia, racism and sexism wouldn't be as prevalent. And I know Lyn wasn't just putting it on for the camera.

We donated the couple of hundred dollars we raised from ticket sales to DYNAMIC so they could have a catch up after disbanding the previous year. And it was really nice that Emma, despite our differences at the time, attended the show, sat in the front row and accepted the cheque on their behalf.

From Joel Creasey's *Thirsty* (Simon & Schuster, 2017) ISBN 9781925310771

Joel Creasey is one of Australia's most popular stand-up comedians, performing to sell-out crowds. He first performed at fifteen and at nineteen earned Best Newcomer at the Melbourne International Comedy Festival. In 2015 he appeared on I'm a Celebrity ... Get Me Out of Here. He was crowned Comedian of the Year at the *GQ* Men of the Year Awards in 2016 and nominated for the Helpmann Award for Best Comedy Performer in 2017. He appears on The Project, The Great Debate, Just for Laughs, SBS's Eurovision and international tours. He was hand-picked to open the late, great Joan Rivers' show. JoelCreasey.com.au.

Go Postal

JILL JONES

A Triptych

Same Love Goes Harder
Serious Wavering
Consummations

Same Love Goes Harder

Crime boy and the ire of Conservatives
is a flop in the big top

Pornography is the critics' tip

I cracked down body-shaming trouble
on the front line

The Ashes a slum
but 'Same Love' 'go harder'

'there's no excuse' for
Air France emergency and alien
pictures a flop a crack down

Sinister reality fake geniuses
and Vettel's engine trouble

'Tweets from angry old white men'
makes the ire go harder

For arms sales and Uber
'couldn't possibly comment'
Go postal go harder

A flop accusation costly error

'Same Love' thousands march make more
to the top of the charts

Survival polls 'hang the Tories'

Gay anthem the power

I cracked the door
and the love goes harder

Serious Wavering

within this dotty sunlight
and gusts of beams on a wall
shadows sway in
queer bevelled *trémulo*
make abstract shape
on ground's blebs and gash tricks

as light without maps
like cosmos winks
like ribbons and motes
inventories to exploit
as mossy tokens wrinkle
a bower with its prism

Consummations

I

the spinning world
     the guttural dark
sounds the skin   & leaves you
     a book of consummations
fresh as rot & queer within

II

in the torn fabric
     the ancient salvage
it's all moving
     clues   charms   throngs
the dearest ground

III

exhale
     between breath bones
no moment more free
     horizon   potent
enough to be touched

———————

Jill Jones has published ten books of poetry, and a number of chapbooks. The latest is *Brink*. 'Consummations' was previously published in a different format in *Brink*, Five Islands Press, 2017. Other recent books include *The Beautiful Anxiety*, which won the Victorian Premier's Prize for Poetry in 2015, and *Breaking the Days*, shortlisted for the 2017 Kenneth Slessor Award. She edited, with Michael Farrell, *Out of the Box: Contemporary Australian Gay and Lesbian Poets*.

Shy Bairns Get Nowt

GUY JAMES WHITWORTH

HOMOSEXUAL HISTORIES CONFERENCE PAPER, NOVEMBER 2017

I grew up in Northumberland in the North East of England. I was a painfully uncomfortable and under-confident child who really struggled. At school I was shy, short, asthmatic and an obvious future homosexual, much to the vicious amusement of the other kids and teachers.

It's a familiar story, I know; 'I was bullied relentlessly'. Basically, think Billy Elliot, but a lot less adorable, with no sense of rhythm, no warm fuzzy ending in sight and the fabulous Julie Walters nowhere to be seen.

To compound my lack of manliness, because of my asthma, I was taken out of all sporting activities, I was literally sent off the playing field and told to just go sit quietly in the art rooms.

Unfortunately, my home life was really no better with a violent ex-military father for whom my lack of manliness was a constant embarrassment.

But even then, to me, gender roles were more of a serving suggestion rather than a recipe to be followed down to the last ingredient. And long before 'passing' became a thing, I struggled to understand why I had to.

I was never male enough, always too girly. I could sometimes pass as a boy child, but never as a future man. Others who celebrated their own easy masculinity could sense the lack of it in me, and they took aim accordingly.

Long before self-esteem became a thing, I struggled to have any.

So just to recap, it was all a bit 'shite' really.

It was art that saved me in so many ways. It was an escape, and it came in many forms. Long before fine art it was in comics, or graphic novels, to give them their fancy name.

And talking of names, back then, my own name gave me grief and I couldn't say the words 'I'm Guy' for years without mumbling or stuttering. The words Guy and gay were too close. Too meaningful, too loaded. Being able to say it now makes me proud. It's a nice name, its camp and pretentious just like me, Guy James Whitworth!

But back then, I would actively avoid any situation where I had to say my own name.

I grew to hate my lack of stereotypical masculinity and I contemplated self-harming and even suicide on a regular basis. My mother knew of my battles and loved me as much as she could to compensate for what I endured. My father knew of my struggles and, I always thought, turned his back on me; but it's only now that I realise he just didn't know how to help and that the time must have been a bit shite for him also.

My maternal grandmother was a bit of a character and a very welcome ally against the outside world. Although she definitely wasn't familiar with what I was going through (I certainly never even heard her say the word gay), I think in a way she got what was happening and tried to give me some tools to help. My self-confidence was so low I rarely spoke and would try to hide myself away in family get-togethers.

However, there was a phrase she would often use and without it, I certainly wouldn't be here.

My grandmother would often use the expression 'Shy bairns get nowt'. And I have clear memories of her saying this directly to me. In Northumberland where I grew up *bairns* means kids or children, and *nowt* means nothing, so what she was saying was shy kids get nothing.

It's still my motto to this very day. It's a mantra I use in situations where I have to make myself do things like public speaking. Even though it's tough for me, I have to make myself heard. There's nothing to be gained by trying to hide at this point, because, well, 'Shy bairns get nowt'.

Isolation is the opposite of community, yet isolation and community can actually both be equally destructive or inspirational. I was happiest when in isolation as a child, when I was alone. In the quiet art rooms of my school I felt safe and I was inspired. When out in the bigger community, that's where I was in danger and often had to run the gauntlet or get the absolute living shit kicked out of me on a daily basis.

I might have been short and asthmatic, but let me tell you when it came to running, when I had to, I could run like the fucking wind!

But you know? Without knowing it, every bully who threw an insult or punch my way, in reality, was placing a tiny piece of fabulous armour on me. Every insult made me that little bit stronger and tougher and contributed towards a future of endless inspiration.

I left school as quickly as I could and went running straight to art school. Finally, other creative types – yay!

But I never actually studied art. Although I said earlier it was art that saved me, I wasn't ready to embrace my salvation quite yet; I had a lot of self-doubt and self-destruction to go through first.

I actually wasn't brave enough to light the fuse on all of that backed up emotional trauma. I just wasn't ready. I needed something safer, so I studied fashion, nice, safe, shallow fashion. I still had decades before I would take my painting seriously.

However, studying fashion did give me a creative kick-start and did take me to London.

It was the late eighties and it was there in London I learnt to finally say my name and peek out from under all that low self-esteem. I actually met other queer people and it was here I got to confirm without a doubt that penises, were indeed, my genitalia of choice!

Now I'd like to play a game; do you all remember that feeling the first time you ever saw a queer person really own what it meant to be queer? Someone who was either so confident in their queerness or so fierce and fabulous in their alternative, fuck-you-I'm-queer-ness that it took your breath away?

Do you remember how that made you feel? For me, it was finally the ability to breathe, and embrace optimism. Those were my glory years. It was a coming out, a coming home. Let me just say, there was a lot of coming, and we'll leave it at that.

Unfortunately, there was no quick fix for the damage done, even now, still, in my late forties I often find myself in situations where I feel my lack of manliness holds me back and I occasionally still suffer from hideous low self-esteem and a fear of the outside world.

However, 'fortune favours the brave' is another one of my favourite sayings and now my struggles are now a lot less life-threatening.

One of my ongoing struggles now, is achieving some kind of recognition in the 'mainstream' and by that I mean straight art world, with constant rejection from both galleries and art prizes as my work is seen as too 'niche' and by that I mean queer. However, it turns out, those years of rejection and ridicule up in the North East left me rather strong and resilient; I'll not be sent off the playing field again, thank you.

The queer element of my work is evident in the models I portray, the colours I use, the forms I paint and in the settings I choose for my sitters. Basically it is inherent to everything I do. I cannot and do not want to change those features of my work.

Because of that queerness, my work now struggles to find its place in the world. Like so many of us, it is too colourful, too bright, too alternative and too fuck-you to find its place easily and without compromise. So you know what I have to do, I just have to change the world.

I may sound quite confident at this point, but if anybody fancied lending a hand for that world changing, I'd appreciate the help.

People who know about the art world tell me that I should embrace my dark side and that I should pull out the demons I faced as a child and put that darkness into my paintings. I paint portraits and I am constantly told my portraits make people too colourful and that safer, more muted colours sell better.

However, fuck that shit, I get to choose the colours in the world that I portray.

What I said earlier about that feeling when you first saw a queer person really own their queerness; well that is the message that I'm channelling into my art. That's what I'm bringing to the world. Unapologetic fierceness, colour, joy, attitude and queer love.

For all the little baby gays still trapped in Northumberland, my paintings are me giving back to the shy, short, strange kids back in whereever the hell it is we all come from. I can't physically bring some fearless and confident queer into that world of the bullied and beaten baby gays, but I can portray that awesome defiant queerness, capture the fabulousness and make it accessible to those that struggle in a way they can recognise and follow out of the darkness of their bullied and abusive childhood.

I came to this party later than I should. I didn't have the confidence to step forward, face my demons and raise my voice until recently. It turns out I needed a safe environment, a supportive partner and good group of mates to give me that push to the front of the stage. But now I'm here I have to clearly state my message: a celebration of diversity, equality and humility. It's visible in my work and it's a message that cannot be ignored. The straight art world can keep turning away as much as it wants, I'll just keep painting and I'll just keep speaking and sooner or later, hopefully my message will be heard and my work will be seen. If people deem it queer art, I'm fine with that, although, when people dismiss it as 'just' queer art, then obviously I still have work to do and the world still needs to be changed.

Again, any help would be appreciated!

The help I normally get, when it comes to support and encouragement normally comes from the queer community. In return it is that part of society that inspires me the most and it is the fair portrayal of that diverse community that challenges and rewards me the most.

However, I do often find that a repetitive *and justified* criticism of my work is that I don't paint women as often as men, and this is true.

I struggle with my artistic relationship with women, I find men easy, so to speak, but women I find complex in a way that I often tussle with. It is often said that a writer can only write convincingly about what they know, and it's the same with painting, I'm simply not at my most confident when painting women, despite growing up with three older sisters and having an amazing set of aunties, and let's not forget my fabulous grandmother, as strong female role models.

I believe that the story of the modern woman is just not mine to tell. I connect easily with lesbians, and there are a few trans models that I had sit for me a few times and I think those paintings are some of my most dynamic; but I fear that when portraying women I am yet just one more man objectifying a woman and that for me to interpret, lay any claim to, or portray their story, is cultural assimilation of a sort and that doesn't sit easy with me. It is an ongoing challenge in my work; but it's one that I am open to and embrace, and certainly not one I'm giving up on. But I do accept the criticism that my portraits of women can sometimes be less adventurous then those of men, and I know that is because of my own creative hesitation.

On the other hand masculinity and the gratuitous depiction of it is right up my alley! I feel very confident to get right up close to that subject. (There was no way of writing this where these statements didn't sound like a double entendre, so I'm just going with it!)

I had an exhibition twelve months ago in Sydney called 'What Maketh a Man', which tackled and challenged the narrow and quite brittle clichés around classic masculinity, especially 'a true man's' physicality. The exhibition was made up of over fifty studies of the male nude. A sportsman, a body builder, a political activist, an investment banker, a dancer and a poet were just a small selection of the brave souls who bared all to help redefine what makes a man under my artistic interpretation.

People are brave and they trust me and I really appreciate that. The show was intended to deconstruct and challenge the concept of modern masculinity, gender roles and sexual politics by literally stripping away all that pretense and artifice.

That project was actually really a celebration of the massive diversity of body shape, age, ability, skin tone and character that go together to make any one of us who we are. All of us are different, all of us are unique and all of us need to embrace our differences if we are really going to thrive and be comfortable with ourselves. Well, I only went and won a bloody award for that show didn't I! I won the Cayte Latta memorial art prize at the LGBTQI honour awards in Sydney.

That exhibition summed up my art practise and the message within my work. I certainly never expected to win an award for that show, Jeez, to be honest I never even expected anyone to turn up and see the show, I never do at any of my exhibitions – remember that low self-worth I mentioned? But lots of people did and that made me very happy. It made me happy for a few reasons, but it mostly made me happy because it meant other people understood what I was trying to do with my work and what I was trying to question and challenge.

As I said earlier, I was never a typical male child, but I think I could have been a much happier child if I'd been given a lot more varied range of role models, and by that I mean physically, emotionally and spiritually. I made a remark earlier about gender roles being more of a serving suggestion than an exact recipe, but really, I believe that wholeheartedly; we need to throw away most ideas about gender role models and outdated, unrealistic and reductive views on masculinity.

And again to talk about that armour that was placed on me by bullies and haters, well it turns out it's actually more of an interchangeable fitted two-piece with accessories and a matching clutch and I can remove any of it easily when needed to resource appropriate softness and vulnerability. Unfortunately, not all men can say that. As other men struggle to become open and free to access emotional authenticity, I, just like a lot of queer men, find those resources ever ready and dependable and a huge help when it comes to mental health and emotional wellbeing.

Another element of the 'What Maketh a Man' project was the larger question of whether classic masculinity is nature or nurture, passed down through generation to generation or individually assumed. I think it is definitely more of the former. I think fathers pass on coping mechanisms to sons; they give them ideals and role models to hide behind – again, physically, emotionally and spiritually.

I count myself incredibly lucky that that didn't really take hold with me and can point to my lack of connection with my father for that good fortune.

For the past few decades I have worked in the field of costume (from managing a costume hire store to working in the art department at Opera Australia) so if anyone knows about hiding behind the external character of a costume it is me. So it makes sense a large part of my art practice is about stripping away unnecessary layers, banishing clichés and trying my best to portray that we are all different, all vulnerable, and that we all have a story to tell no matter how awkward, individual or unconventional we are. The idea of masculinity, and how we need to pass behind a convincing masculine façade, shapes a lot of habits and behavioural practices of men and those around them, whether we like it or not, and this is what my work challenges.

What if I'd never been bullied? What if it hadn't taken me decades of squandered, unproductive time to find the confidence to exhibit my work, what if my alternative creative queerness had been accepted and encouraged by the community I grew up in? Who would I be now and what would I be able to do differently?

Those questions sadden me and it's my biggest regret that I'll never know the answers; however, all of that said, I'm now in an awesome place and I know and appreciate that.

The past twelve months have seen a bit of a steady, and very welcome, climb in how my work has been received, with me winning my first ever art award, The Obi Art Prize up in Queensland and also scoring my first ever public speaking gig at Queer Stories in Sydney. I'm in a good place and I appreciate that, statistically, many from similar backgrounds to myself either don't make it, or survive as the walking wounded and don't get to fully process the struggles they went through.

I'm one of the lucky ones, I get to process, I get to create, and I get a platform to communicate what happened in my past and celebrate my present.

The armour that was placed on me years ago falls off me now easily at the pull of an imaginary string whenever needed and I have no fear at letting people in to see my vulnerable and non-typically masculine, awkward self. I am still that short and weird kid from Northumberland, but now I judge myself on my own terms and no one else's. I can look at the self-portraits that I paint of myself, stand back, and see someone in those paintings that I would like to get to know and someone that I like. And although I still see glimmers of that under-confident kid, I now can say my name with pride and confidence.

My name is Guy James Whitworth and please remember, shy bairns get nowt.

_____

Guy James Whitworth was born under a wandering star in the industrial North East of England. Over the years he has tried his hand at many trades (model, costume designer, performer, poet, illustrator). Guy lives in Surry Hills and works primarily as a portrait artist. Guy's solo exhibitions have been a huge hit with the public, collectors and critics, with ABC online calling him 'one of the most promising and collectible artists' around at the moment. Guy's painting *Miren* graces the cover of this edition of *Bent Street*. www.guyjameswhitworth.com

The Child's Best Interests?

GENINE HOOK

Queer families and exclusionary marriage activism

I am a wholehearted supporter of marriage equality in Australia. I have voted YES in the postal survey despite its problematic political and financial implications. In this paper, though, I critique the queer framing of elements of the marriage equality debate from the perspective of sole parent families; specifically, the problematic discourses the marriage debate perpetuated about sole parent families. In her book, *The Perils of Marriage Equality*, (2015) Katherine Franke questions the process of normalization of marriage equality, and advocates for 'recognition and respect for a variety of marriage and family forms' (p. 223). Franke is critical of a marriage equality position which 'too often depended on equating state recognition of relationships with legitimacy and on valuing marriage in a way that denigrated non-marital family forms' (p. 113). This can leave non-married parents as constituted as lacking in the 'something special' that we tag on marriage, this perpetuates stigma, pathology and injury in relation to both children and intimates within kinship relations beyond the marital code. According to Australian Bureau of Statistics (ABS, 2016), there are 959,543 sole parent families which make up 15.8% of all Australian families. 81.8% of these sole parent families are headed by females. Sole parents and their families are beyond the marital code and as a sole parent of fourteen years, I experience much of the marriage equality discourse as affective violence. In some ways this affective violence is more deeply felt as it has been sent from my 'home' team; queer and alternative kinship.

Sole Parenthood as Shameful Nonplace

In 2004, I become a sole parent of an eight month old baby, dumped out of a ten year marriage, blindsided, dumb and discarded. Butler (2004) calls this a 'nonplace' – a conflicted space that didn't equate to anything I knew or had experienced;

> [t]hese are nonplaces in which one finds oneself in spite of oneself; indeed, these are nonplaces where recognition, including self-recognition, proves precarious if not elusive, in spite of one's best efforts to be a subject in some recognizable sense (p. 108).

My reaction to becoming a sole parent is one of shame and vulnerability. Michael Warner (1999), states that shame 'attaches not to doing, but to being; not to conduct, but to status' (p. 28). In being dumped, my status changed to 'being' a sole parent. Warner links this sense of shame to 'a hierarchy of respectability' (Warner, 1999, p. 49). He nominates marriage as a hierarchical social norm that denotes respectability. This hierarchy exists because 'marriage sanctifies some couples at the expense of others. It is selective legitimacy … if you don't have it, you and your relations are less worthy' (Warner, 1999, p. 82). Although Warner is discussing same-sex marriage, the point remains relevant for sole parents whose families 'don't have it' (marriage) and therefore are often seen as lacking legitimacy. Having a new-born baby as a sole parent felt, to me, like a slide down the hierarchy of respectability. I experienced a sense of shame for myself and my child as a 'less worthy/legitimate/valued' family.

Sole Parenthood as Diverse Queer and Alternative Kinship

Queer theory shifting away from its home of sexuality and LGBTIQ issues can support an exploration of diversity in families. In my work I consider the experiences of sole parents and their families; the joyfulness and rich nature of sole parent families. It is not a common discourse. Queer theory's usefulness is to contest heteronormativity and to challenge the 'naturalness' of the hetero – including the expectation that the 'ideal' family structure is a 'nuclear family' that only allows for a masculine male heterosexual parent, a feminine female heterosexual parent and their shared biological children. In my research I argue that sole parents are queering the heteronormative family. Sole parents traverse through and across lines of gendered binaries in relation to feminine mothering and masculine fathering in a way that is foundational to the privilege of the hetero nuclear family. I argue that exploring the experiences of sole parent families can shift ways in which we constitute kinship and contests the prescribed nature of the nuclear family.

Problematic Queer Attacks on Sole Parenthood

Ann Crittenden's (2001) book *The Price of Motherhood* positions motherhood as the most important and least valued job in the world and regards nuclear families as ideal because they are, 'proving every day that two parents are better than one' (p. 119). Similarly, Anthony Giddens (1998) rehearses debates of the disintegrating family in his book *The Third Way*. Giddens (1998) refers to the 'breakdown' of the family due to increased divorce rates and calls for a 'restructuring of parenthood' (p. 95). He then goes further to argue that sole parent families are at a disadvantage economically but also from 'inadequate parental attention and lack of social ties' (Giddens, p. 93). Associate Professor Paula Gerber (2010) argues that it is in the best interests of children for same-sex marriage to be legally recognised. She argues that a 'negative impact' occurs when children from heterosexual families are privileged through access to the stable and nurturing environment of marriage. Gerber (2010) states that children who do not 'enjoy the recognition and support that comes with marriage may suffer psychological harm as a result of the prohibition on their parents marrying' (p. 33). This is a brief glimpse of academic discourses that constitute sole parenting. I am keen not to reproduce and participate in negative discourses relating to sole parent families. I understand them as not only problematically descriptive but also productively reinscribing troubling parameters of the 'ideal' family. I cite these few examples in order to illustrate how negative social discourses about sole parents continues to proliferate, and is reflected in social policies; this repetitive loop becomes normative, a 'citational legacy' (Butler, 1993a, p. 171).

Challenging 'The Best Interests of the Children'

As one of these sole parents queer writers and marriage advocates are discussing, I find it very politically and affectively difficult to align my support for marriage equality to the associated position of marriage as something 'in the best interests of children'. Paula Gerber (2012) wrote in the Drum (ABC) that 'children who are raised by married parents (be they same-sex or opposite-sex) benefit from the legal and social status granted to their parents. Quoting national and international research Gerber states that, 'All of these studies demonstrate that it is in the best interests of children to allow same-sex couples to marry'. Here, the argument for marriage equality is that marriage, in whatever form, is in the best interests of the children.

The official marriage equality organization takes up this position in support of a YES vote. It advises that in response to the question from people who may question voting yes:

> *Don't children do best with a mother and a father?*
> Decades of research confirms that children do best in a family with loving parents, regardless of whether those parents are straight or gay. And LGBTI people have been successfully parenting in Australia, including adopting, for many years. Marriage equality won't change this but will offer stronger security and belonging to all families.

Does it seem fair to exclude some children from the security that comes from marriage?

(sourced from
http://www.equalitycampaign.org.au/conversations)

I am disappointed and strongly opposed to this marriage is 'in the best interests of children' argument. I don't support a position that effectively puts forward one person's rights, at the expense of another. It seems problematic to argue for difference to be validated while, at the same time, diminishing the difference of others. 'For the sake of the children' tends to pass the negative conventions down the line and I think lessens the clarity and ethics of care that I have associated with the queer activist community. It is un-ethical for one group who are arguing for respect and space for their construct of 'durable intimacy' (Berlant 2011, p. 3), to shift the profound threat towards another construct of togetherness. I also want to argue against constructing a position that demands justifying, explaining or legitimating kinship or familial relations. I suggest that this position to support marriage equality is similar to a 'tolerance' argument, that you show tolerance for difference, but shape it to illustrate a lack of 'tolerance' for an alternative way of living and being.

Challenging 'Straight' Arguments for Queer Concerns

Perhaps my reticence towards elements of the marriage equality debate is the tendency towards straight/conventional arguments for queer concerns. It is the 'suffusion of the ordinary with fantasy' (Berlant, 2011, p. 14), that I feel is central to the marriage debate and my response here. The ordinary sense of family and intimacy is bound to the fantasy of the 'good life'. My concern is that in the current marriage equality debate, the re-shaping of the 'good life' which has a legacy from heteronormativity, shifts towards sex-same *coupledom*. This re-shaping broadens who can access this construction of the 'good life', but it does so at the expense of those individuals living their lives outside of coupledom whom it excludes. I argue that as a sole parent, my familial conditions only become damaging when regulatory norms and social discourse *exclude me* and grind into my experiences of my 'good life'. This othering of 'sole parenting', making it 'not quite right', illegitimate, I suggest, is a form of exclusionism that a queer position should be theoretically and politically reticent to take.

Response-able Queer, in Closing

Marriage is one way of framing and experiencing kinship and intimacy:

> One might point out that all objects/scenes of desire are problematic, in that investments in them and projections onto them are less about them, than about what cluster of desires and affects we can manage to keep magnetized to them (Berlant, 2011, p. 24).

The cluster of desires and affects that we project into the marital state are not exclusively found/felt there. The utility of queer theory is the capacity to interrogate the experiences of a category whilst questioning the category itself. As Youdell (2011) reminds us, categories are useful tools to investigate experiences because to 'identify inequalities is to call up a range of categorizations of identity' (p. 22). I am aware of the risk that refusing one regulatory norm can re-instate another, or as Youdell (2011) states, a slip into transformative narratives 'that call up one regulatory discourse to displace another, and which effect one set of subjectivations to replace another' (p. 116). It is this displacement that concerns me in relation to queer positions and kinship and the exclusion that can be embedded into elements of the marriage equality discourse. 'In the face of what appears, we must ask what disappears' (Ahmed, 2006, p. 90). I suggest that the kinship and familial bonds of sole parent families have disappeared within the marriage equality 'in the best interests of children' discourse, which is an example of ways in which 'the discursive condition of social recognition precedes and conditions the formation of the subject' (Butler, 2013, p. 19).

Queer activism and theoretical frameworks have been mobilized because of exclusions. They must now be responsible and responsive to how the term and its activist potentials towards subversion are mobilized within the development of Australian marriage moving forward.

References

ABS. (2016), *2016 Census QuickStats. Website.* Accessed: 10/10/17. Retrieved from: http://www.censusdata.abs.gov.au/census_services/ getproduct/census/2016/quickstat/036.

Ahmed, S., (2006), *Queer Phenomenology*, Durham, Duke University Press.

Berlant, L., (2011), *Cruel Optimism*, Durham, Duke University Press.

Braidotti, R., (2011), *Nomadic subjects: embodiment and sexual difference in contemporary feminist theory*, 2nd Ed. New York, Columbia University Press.

Butler, J., (2004), *Undoing Gender*, New York, Routledge.

Butler, J., (2005), *Giving an account of oneself*, New York, Fordham University Press.

Butler, J., (2013), Critically Queer, In, D.E. Hall & A. Jagose, (Eds), *The Routledge queer studies reader*, London, Routledge, p.18-31.

Crittenden, A., (2001), *The Price of Motherhood: Why the most important job in the world is still the least valued*, New York, Henry Holt and Co.

Franke, K., (2015), *The Perils of Marriage Equality*, New York, NYU Press.

Gerber, P., (2010), The best interests of children in same-sex families, *Law in Context*, Vol. 28, No. 1, pp. 28-42.

Gerber, Paula (2012), *Marriage Equality, Myths and Misconceptions*, Retrieved from: http://www.abc.net.au/news/2012-05-15/gerber-marriage-equality/4010980.

Giddens, A., (1998), *The Third Way: The renewal of social democracy*, Cambridge, Polity Press.

Talburt, S., (2000), *Subject to identity: Knowledge, sexuality, and academic practices in higher education*, Albany, State University of New York Press.

Warner, M., (1999), *The trouble with normal: Sex, politics, and the ethics of queer life*, New York, Free Press.

Youdell, D., (2011), *School Trouble: Identity, Power and Politics in Education*, London, Routlege.

Genine Hook studied Sociology and Education (Secondary) at Monash University and a PhD at the Faculty of Education at Monash University in May 2015. Her thesis explored sole parents at Australian universities and was awarded the Vice-Chancellor's Commendation for Thesis Excellence in 2015. Her first book, *Sole Parent Students and Higher Education: Gender, Policy and Widening Participation*, was published by Palgrave Macmillan (UK) in July 2016. She works at The University of New England teaching Sociology: Family and Children in Society; Youth and Delinquency; and Mixed Methods. Her research considers gender, higher education, family-based violence and queering familial norms.

Butterfluck | GUY JAMES WHITWORTH

Becoming Mick Sheehan

TINA HEALY

Mick sat dangling his feet in the waters of the Pond, a secluded billabong fed by the waters of Concongella Creek. It was sufficiently far from the road that the sounds of horse and cart were inaudible. Only the occasional growling of a motor truck on its way to Ballarat could be heard. Looking down at the reflection of his face, he noticed how the blue grey leaves of the gum trees behind him seemed to move and shimmer in the ripples made by his toes. He tried to match his name to the face that looked back at him from the water.

In his mind he held his name. He turned it this way, then that. No matter how hard he tried, this piece of the puzzle just didn't fit. Mick. Turn it this way. Mick. Turn it that way. Mick. You may as well call a sheep a bloody duck. Mick wore his name like a shirt on backwards. He couldn't put words to how he felt. Like an itch but no rash. Like when you put your shoes on the wrong feet. In frustration, he kicked the face in the water, grabbed his dusty satchel, and headed off to school.

State Primary School number 362 was one of six structures that sat on the Wimmera Plain that defined the township of Quartz Reef. Next to the one-room school was a tiny teacher's residence that sidled up to it for company. Further down the road sat a church dressed in weathered boards that continued to peel in the persistent heat of summer. Thin, rusted sheets of corrugated iron stayed on the roof, more from habit than as a result of the few nails that remained. A flat sheet of tin crucified to a rickety wooden frame announced that this was St Mary's Catholic Church. The cow that fed on the long grass nearby cared little for religion, however, it enjoyed the shade offered, and donated a large turd in appreciation.

ℭ

Mick creaked his way a step at a time toward the enormous schoolhouse door that kept the heated breeze from cooking the juvenile ingredients within. He pulled the handle hard and a gust of warm air escaped. A stronger surge of hot air muscled in ahead of him flapping the covers of twenty-nine dog-eared books, sitting on twenty-nine dilapidated desks. A thirtieth desk sat empty, brooding at the very front of the classroom waiting for Mick. Again.

Godfrey Lawrence Howard stood at the blackboard. The children rarely called their teacher by that name. They called him The Ferret, as it better reflected his slight build and pinched face. The Ferret stood, tapping his cane rhythmically against his thigh.

Mick stood at the back of the class. His hands began to sting and burn in anticipation. As he walked up the centre aisle, he could feel the sneers of the boys on his left, and hear the smothered snickers of the girls on his right. The school had a motley mixture of ages and heights, but a strict divide existed between the genders. Boys baked on the west side of the room, because their windows faced a sun whose heat dropped birds from their branches. The girls sat on the east side protected from the direct sun. Occasionally the steamed odour of unwashed socks and sweaty armpits would waft from the boys as they cooked on the other side.

Mick reached the front of the room. The Ferret smiled and grabbed his arm. He held it out with his left hand, and swooped the cane downwards with his right. A loud whack resonated around the room. The whole class jumped. Mick cried out and squeezed his hand between his thighs to try and numb the pain. The Ferret demanded that Mick present his other hand. Mick tried to be somewhere else in his mind.

But he was blasted back into the moment as white pain leapt from his outstretched hand. The Ferret turned him around to face the class, and used the cane to prod him toward the empty desk. A few boys smirked at him. Most of the girls looked away, except for Sheila who held his gaze with those big gentle eyes.

ɞ

The Ferret spent the rest of the morning droning the same stupid lessons he'd been teaching for years, but Mick was too angry to listen. Finally the lunch break came and Mick made his way outside with the other kids. A mob of boys joined Moira Jones and her footy and headed toward the top yard. 'Kick it here Jonesy!' Paddy yelled. A group of older girls ignored Sheila and headed for the asphalted area on the shaded side of the school. There were chalked hopscotch games still there from yesterday. Some of the younger children drifted toward the seesaw, braving the heat of the wood that seared their backsides.

Mick waited at the foot of the steps with Sheila's dog Stretch. The twist in her leg made the task a bit difficult, but eventually Sheila joined Mick and Stretch and they made their way to the shady green canopy of the peppercorn trees. This was their safe place where they talked every lunchtime and sometimes after school. The grass was always soft and lush from the nearby rainwater tank that leaked all year round.

'Just wait! One day I'm gonna tell that bloody Ferret what I think!' said Mick. Sheila just nodded. She and Mick would often sit on the banks of the Pond, close to the creek that wound its way through the scrub at the back of their family farms. They would throw twigs in the water and Stretch would happily leap in and fetch them each time. Mick was a great storyteller and Sheila was a good listener.

ɞ

Too soon, the school bell sounded and they made their way back to class. The Ferret stood impatiently at the door. He growled at Moira to go and wash her face and hands, and told Sheila to get a move on. As

Mick walked past, the Ferret smirked. Mick went to say something, but was distracted by other events that unfolded.

Stretch reckoned he was a really good judge of character. He heard The Ferret growl at Sheila. So while The Ferret looked at Mick, Stretch crept quietly up to The Ferret's shoes, and pissed on them. By the time the teacher realised what had happened, Stretch had bolted for Brown's paddock, where he sat and smiled. The Ferret took his shoes off and washed them under a tap. He picked up a stone and threw it at the dog, but it landed twenty feet short. He put his sodden shoes back on his feet, and squelched his way back to the front of classroom. A small pool of water formed next to his shoes as he stood there. He glared at Sheila. As the owner of the dog, he would have enjoyed making her pay for his humiliation. But he knew that was a line he could not cross. Yet.

The children smothered their laughter behind stone faces. Except for Tommo Reynolds whose laughter echoed from the rear of the room.

'Stand up Reynolds!' yelled the Ferret.

Tommo slowly stood. At fifteen years-old he was already the size of most adults. His was tall and built like a Mallee bull, so none of the other kids commented on his darker complexion.

'Get up here Reynolds!' The Ferret pointed with his cane at a spot in front of the blackboard, but away from the puddle.

Mick boiled. It seemed he was caned most days. He admired Tommo and looked up to him. Not just physically, but also because he had this inner calm, a strength that people like the Ferret would never understand. He wished he could be like Tommo, but that inner voice would always whisper, 'You're worthless. You're chipped crockery mate. You're not even a real bloke.' And then the anger would turn inward and he'd hate himself. Lost in his own thoughts, he hadn't noticed that the Ferret had made Tommo bend over. The Ferret walked down the aisle, past Mick's desk, so he could get a run-up with the cane.

There are moments in life when our hearts take control, and we act in ways we could never imagine. Those times when you look back, shake your head and say, 'I don't know how I did that, but Wow!' Mick saw the Ferret hold up the cane and begin his run. It was his mate up there. He knew the pain Tommo was about to feel, because Mick felt it every other day. Mick yelled out, 'No!' In the slightest of movements his right foot moved from under the desk to the centre of the aisle. The Ferret wasn't watching. He had eyes only for his target.

Children talked about it in hushed admiration for years. The legend grew as the story aged. No one could remember who it was that stuck their foot out just at the right moment. But certain images will be etched into their minds forever. The Ferret had tripped, slipped, then done a watery skid toward the stunned Tommo, who had a second or two to glance back in horror at the terrified face of the oncoming man. The Ferret stuck his foot in the puddle next to Tommo, who ducked just in time. The Ferret screamed and somersaulted over Tommo, through the teacher's desk, and headfirst into the blackboard.

No one moved at first. The Ferret was slumped motionless behind the splintered devastation of the desk. Sheila was the first one to move. She checked out the teacher and found he was bruised but alive. She called out to Moira, 'Go get your mum, Jonesy, and tell her to bring her buggy just in case!' Then she sat down next to Tommo who was seated on the floor. 'You alright?' she said. Tommo just nodded.

Sheila's eyes searched the room for Mick, but he was long gone.

༄

Sheila found Mick some time later at the Pond. Mick's gaze was focused on two sticks with a remarkable resemblance to a broken cane. They floated there with his thoughts, on their way to the Wimmera River. In his heart he wished he could join them on their way out of Quartz Reef, past the Grampians, and into a future where he could be himself. But at least he'd had a win. Sheila joined him there on the bank. She leaned forward and saw the smile on his face.

'Did ya see him go arse over turkey in the puddle?' she asked.

'Yep,' he replied. And the sound of their laughter echoed like a pair of kookaburras, through the leafy canopy, beyond the little town, and on to the far horizon at the edge of the Wimmera Plains.

This chapter is the beginning of a fictional piece built around a snippet of truth I was told by Dad's sister years ago, before I came out as trans. They lived in rural Victoria in the 1930s. She said they had a cousin who dressed as male in public, but was allowed to dress as female on the farm. They found him hanging in the barn dressed as a girl when he was a teenager. My story is built around that event, and written to honour the transgirl that died and the many trans kids that struggle today.

Tina Healy is an advocate, peer support worker and an elder in the transgender community. She is a dad to her children, grandma to her grandchildren, and just 'Tina' to her community. Tina was co-coordinator of Gender Diversity Australia, and is currently co-coordinator of Alphabet Soup - a peer support group in Melbourne and regional Victoria. Now semi-retired, she is following her passion as a writer.

Untold Stories | APRIL WHITE

One Weekend in October

JEAN TAYLOR

Like Cinderella we're getting ready to go to the Ball – the Coming Back Out Ball at the Melbourne Town Hall, that is.

Ardy is wearing her 'This Is What An Old Lesbian Looks Like' teeshirt she bought at the recent Old Lesbians Organising for Change Gathering in Tampa, Florida. And I've opted for my Frida Kahlo print pants she made me in her sewing class, plus a green singlet showing under my orange top. It's not till we're outside and getting in the taxi – I've had an arthritic flare-up in my right knee and am on meds to be able to walk with a minimum of pain otherwise we'd be catching the tram as usual – that I notice that we're both wearing our, not matching fortunately, brightly coloured cardies.

The next day, when our photo appears on Facebook, someone mentions we look like Kath and Kel in the episode where they spent their holidays at the Tullamarine airport. I embrace this concept without a qualm.

I have been to any number of lesbian dances and have helped organise a number of Women's Balls, two a year at the San Remo Ballroom and the St Kilda Town Hall, during the late '80s and early '90s to keep the Women's Liberation Building open and accessible with any number of the womyn's bands providing the live music to keep us bopping all evening long. But I have never been able to afford to attend the gay male organised extravaganzas over the previous years. Till now. I'm here because this one is well subsidised as part of Seniors Week, and is free to members of the LGBTI community over 65.

It doesn't take us long to find our table up the back of that large hall which slowly fills with LGBTIQ community members as we gradually get used to our very sumptuous surroundings and catch up with the lesbians we know for a chat. I'm here for a couple of reasons. Ardy has been a lesbian consultant, for want of a better word, in the lead up to the Ball and her photo has appeared in some of the publicity as well as the program; and the well-known and loved lesbian entertainers in the line-up are not to be missed.

I especially enjoy the opportunity to hear the Yorta Yorta opera singer Deborah Cheetham once again and singer-songwriter Robyn Archer does a great job as the emcee. I also like watching Kathleen McGuire conducting the orchestra on stage. I give a standing ovation to the Performing Older Women's Circus, which I had founded in 1995 for womyn over 40, strutting their acrobatic stuff on stage. I take great delight in Ardy's few words into the microphone for all to hear. Much to my surprised delight, the food is much better than I'd expected and someone keeps topping up my glass with sparkling all evening.

What's not to like, I ask myself, as the entertainment keeps on coming in small sound and movement bytes for hours till there is hardly enough time for the dancing at the end. But dance everyone does on the very crowded dance floor. Except for me with my bung knee. Me, who has danced my feet off at every lesbian dance and Women's Ball since the 1970s. I'm barely able to hobble let alone do anything like lift my feet and twirl to the music, a painful ending to what has proved to be an evening full of fun and frivolity – more than ably organised by the very-gay-in-his-six-inch-stilettos-and-smart-black-suit, Tristan Meecham, whom we meet up with as we're sitting on a bench outside waiting for our Uber ride to take us home at close to midnight.

The following day, 8 October, is International Lesbian Day, and I wear the same clothes to the Lesbian Tea Dance that afternoon to celebrate the 25th anniversary of the Matrix Guild established in 1992 by and for lesbians over 40. This time Ardy and I are able to drive and give a friend who lives in North Fitzroy a lift with her walker to the Preston Shire Hall. The Matrix Guild Seniors Dance is a much more modest affair, as lesbian events have traditionally been over these past several decades, because we do not have the disposable income and access to resources of the gay males. But no less full of dancing and conviviality and fun for that.

A small grant has enabled the collective to cover costs and provide finger food, including cheese platters, plenty of fruit, a couple of pavlovas and dozens of vegan gluten-free cupcakes, plus coffee and tea. A loop of digital photos is displayed on the screen against one wall, with several photos of myself at various stages of my life over the past couple of decades. We don't win any of the fundraising raffle prizes, but as a founding member of Matrix and active for many years, I make a speech recapping the beginning stages of how the Matrix Guild came to be set up in Victoria and describe some of the fundraisers we members organised to raise money in the early days.

Again, and for the first time in living memory at a lesbian dance, I am unable to groove along to the non-stop dance music with a variety of digitalised music to please every taste. But strangely enough this doesn't bother me as much as I'd thought it would, because I find myself in one interesting conversation after another as these lesbian friends I've known and been around, workshopped and demonstrated with over many years, sit down in the chairs next to mine and catch up with me about our news.

One weekend in October and what a time to have a crook knee! But thank heavens for small mercies, because at least I was able to be there and experience two quite different but equally enjoyable events in our lesbian seniors' calendar.

Jean Taylor is a radical lesbian feminist writer and political activist based on Wurundjeri country in Melbourne. She has been actively engaged in the Women's Liberation Movement and lesbian feminist activism since the 1970s and has written many novels, plays, short stories and non-fiction on these and other subjects. Jean's published work can be found on www.dykebooks.com.

Slightly Foxed

ASHLEY SIEVWRIGHT

EXCERPT FROM A NOVEL-IN-DEVELOPMENT

The phrase, *What the fuck am I doing here?* is one that most of us have
uttered at one time or another through our lives. For Alex, getting out
of a car bum first and realizing that he was half-way to completely off
his tits on MDMA, putrefying in the same clothes he'd been wearing for
two days straight, and about to attend the funeral of somebody else's
grandfather, it was definitely one of those moments.

He stood up into a cold sea breeze, which annoyingly and somewhat
unfairly seemed not to sober him up but to merely underline how off
his tits he actually was. His drug hangover from last night was still there,
but alongside this he was aware of the new pill doing its work, upping
the bid against the hangover. He had secretly self-medicated on the
drive to the cemetery and now he was, in general, fucked up. His heart
was pounding in his chest as if pumping his blood through his organs
was some sort of dragon-boat race or something.

Bec, used to this sort of thing from him and not at all willing to
pander to it, got out of the front passenger seat and said only, 'Try to be
normal,' out the side of her mouth. Drew came around the front of the
car. He had produced a black suit jacket from somewhere and put it
over his jeans and light grey jumper. He buttoned it up with one hand
and stretched the other out to Bec. She stepped towards him and took
his hand, then they moved onto the gravel path into the cemetery and

took off at a mournful pace. They looked like models, Alex thought. They were also, he noted, in step. For a moment he thought they made the most lovely couple ever, and he felt a wave of love and warmth and affection for them. Then he hated them. Then he felt horny for them, but that, he supposed, was the drugs.

He realized that he was standing by the car like the big, black, half-fucked-up, reeking gooseberry that he was. He muttered a quick 'Fuck' and considered climbing back into Drew's car, lying down on the backseat so nobody could see him, and just dragon-boating there until they came back and drove him away. At that moment it felt like a perfectly feasible thing to do, and he had actually turned back to the car – but it was too late. An older man, comfortably rotund, in a dark blue unbuttoned suit jacket, with an expression that was dry-eyed but properly bland and respectful appeared at his arm.

'Are you going up?' the man asked. Alex, flustered, turned to the car then back to the man – the backseat escape was no longer a possibility. He put a brave face on it, but then, realizing his expression was probably a bit intense and inappropriate in the circumstances, he dropped the sides of his mouth and tilted his head in an exaggerated parody of sadness. *Fuck. What was he doing? Mime? Keep a lid on it, fuckwit.*

He fumbled his sunglasses from the pocket of his inappropriate leather jacket and shoved them on his face to hide his wigged-out eyes.

'Yes,' he said.

The man must have presumed Alex to be in a heightened state of grief.

'I know,' he said. 'I know.'

He put his hand to the small of Alex's back and with his other hand indicated the gravel path up to the cemetery. Alex stepped off in the direction indicated. He concentrated on walking and not jittering. If things weren't bad enough, somehow he had now become the chief mourner for a man he didn't know.

೦ಙ

Alex stared across to the woman standing at the side of the grave in what could be considered the prime mourning position. The most obvious thing about her, even from this distance, was that she had evidently had an absolutely enormous amount of plastic surgery. Her face was flat and smooth and looked as hard as a beetle's back. Her mouth was dragged out at each side and her nose had been whittled down to a shaving of soap with two outward facing nostrils.

Apart from the extraordinary face, she was extremely small – the smallness of someone who has shrunk considerably. She wore a very big black A-line coat with a rather ostentatious orange-brown fur collar that moved in the breeze like a sleek fox making off across the paddock. Her arms were clad in black skin-tight sleeves, her legs in skin-tight trousers or perhaps even leggings. The sheer voluminous nature of the coat emphasized the skinniness of the legs and arms and made them look like burnt matchsticks.

But there was something, even as old and thin as she was, that was extraordinarily vivid about her. She wore very big, round, black-framed eye-glasses, so perfectly round that they didn't quite look real, but could feasibly have been authentic 60s mod. On her fingers and wrists, and around her neck and in her ears were innumerable rings and bracelets and necklaces and earrings. Generally they seemed to be of jet and jade and perhaps amber – that was the palette. There were no gemstones that Alex could see, as such, which allowed her to get away with lips and nails which were beautifully, immaculately deep red.

She was the widow, presumably – although apparently the dead man was a number of husbands in the past – and therefore Drew's gran. What a fantastic grandmother, Alex thought, with a wild rush of love for all these people he was seeing – Drew's family and family friends. He felt closer to Drew the more he saw of the people in his life, as if something was leeching from them to him, some secret knowledge, some extra special kinship. He stole a look at Drew. He was still. His head was bent, examining his hands. He appeared deeply affected. But something in his calm suggested to Alex that he was somewhere else in his mind, just behaving properly for the family. He was, Alex saw, picking at his nails.

Alex turned back to the widow. He was fascinated by her, and feeling – feeling sorry for her ... for her loss, perhaps, or for all those procedures, for a lifetime of wanting a different face, for having been through so very many husbands, for being so unlucky in love. The phrase resonated. *Unlucky in love. Oh yes. Yes.* He knew all about being unlucky in love.

He felt a sudden strong shock of kinship with this old stick thin Joan Rivers widow-woman, and he found tears oozing out of his eyes, dripping off his bottom eyelashes and sploshing onto his cheeks from behind his dark glasses.

It was at this moment that the tide broke and he was consumed by a flood of feelings. A great sad soak of them. He allowed himself to wallow in it, in them, and felt oddly elated by his decision to let it wash over him – just wash over him – the sheer hopeless futility of it all – of love. Of life. Of everything. There was a beauty in it – letting yourself be immersed. Letting yourself feel it.

Oh God he was so out of it.

At this pivotal point, tears on his cheeks, Alex noticed a change in tenor to whatever the priest-guy was saying. Things, it appeared, were coming to an end. They were to be released from this graveside into the wild wide blue unknown. The mourners became less focused on the open grave. They turned to each other. They began milling around. Alex turned to Drew's uncle, his tour guide to this particular funeral, took his hand and squeezed it warmly.

'Thank you,' he said with immense depth of feeling and a kind smile.

He then walked purposefully towards Bec and Drew. He kissed Bec quickly and directly on the lips, then turned to Drew and also kissed him full on the lips. They weren't long kisses, and there was no tongue (of course – this was a funeral), but he did put one of his hands to the back of Drew's neck where he could finger that double swirl of almost invisible hair. When he pulled back Drew was smirking at him.

What was he doing? He didn't care.

He turned from the smirk and made a bee-line for the widow. If he was aware of a noise from Bec, some hiss of words to his rear, perhaps his name, it didn't register and certainly not enough to stop him. If there were odd glances from Drew's relatives, if people stepped out of his way as he moved through the crowd, he didn't notice. It didn't matter. He reached the widow and without a word enfolded her in an enormous hug. He felt her twig-thin limbs hug him back. He buried his nose in the foxy-fur of the collar of her coat and took a big sniff of the old-fashioned floral perfume that it seemed deeply infused with. It occurred to him in that moment that it would be wonderful if that was how foxes actually smelled – like Chanel No.5.

He disengaged from the hug but held the old woman's shoulders. He set her back a little from him and looked at her with what he hoped was an expression of sadness and a sort of solidarity of feeling, but he realized at the last minute that she couldn't see his eyes and so he nodded with a sense of sadness and solidarity instead.

'You're so great,' he gushed. 'You're just so great.'

The old woman nodded, and her stretched lips stretched wider – was it a smile? – but she said nothing. In his current frame of mind the regal, stately nature of her response seemed utterly perfect to him. They were so simpatico, he thought. She got it. She got him. The sheer enormity of their moment of connection threated to overcome Alex completely.

But at that moment, the tipping point as it were, Bec appeared at his elbow with the kill-joy alacrity of the designated driver. With a nod and a close-lipped smile at the widow that said, 'I'm sorry for your loss – and for him' in equal measures, she somehow manoeuvred Alex's arm off the widow's shoulder and underneath her own where she clamped it to her side with the sort of iron grip he was sure professional wrestlers had a name for. She then turned him on his heel and smartly led him away from the graveside and back down the gravel path towards the car.

'Well,' she said out the side of her mouth, 'Thanks for keeping it normal.'

03

The wind off the bay was chill, and Alex flipped up the collar of the coat Drew had loaned him. It felt new and soft and smelled not of

Drew — neither of the too-ripe cologne he wore or the sour-sweet scent of his sweat when he didn't bother with it — but, disappointingly, merely clean. It was sexless and void. His mother was too organized for it to smell like anything else. Alex had only met her two days before but he already knew this about her. What was the point of wearing Drew's clothes if he couldn't get a whiff of Drew off them?

The day after the wake, Alex had unzipped his Le Coq Sportif bag and found that he had not precisely packed appropriately for the trip. True, he had only arrived home a bare fifteen minutes before Drew and Bec were due to pick him up, still tripping from the night before and still, mostly, dressed, but what had made him pack a half dozen pair of clean underpants and socks and nothing else except his toothbrush?

He had remembered to pack the books, though — those thirteen paperbacks. They were, after all, the whole point of this trip. Well, he had thought they were. There turned out to be that funeral of an old man he didn't even know and all the attendant blah-blah. The thirteen paperbacks were, at the moment, in a canvas bag hooked over his forearm.

He felt better this morning, two mornings after the funeral. He felt more himself — perhaps the massively hungover version of himself, but still undeniably himself. He was feeling hangover-moody and a bit emotionally fragile, and found his current mode of transport perfectly fitted that mindset — he, Drew and Bec were on the ferry across the mouth of Port Phillip Bay from Queenscliff to Sorrento.

They stood on the top deck of the ferry, open to the slate grey winter sky. Drew and Bec were huddled together alongside the blue cover of the massive twin exhausts at the rear of the deck which was warm. Bec stood with her back against the warmth and Drew, chivalrously, stood on the windward side with his arms around her. Alex had looked once and then away, and nothing would make him look back. He stood instead at the side railing, gripping it in fact, and looked steely eyed and focused at the land they were chugging away from, scanning it for recognizable features.

He could see Queenscliff behind them, and perhaps the tip of Drew's parents' house up on the hill just across from the church, although there was a large cypress tree in the way and it was obscured. Plus he wasn't sure he had the right spot.

And the cemetery. That was where? Half way down to Point Lonsdale. He could see a lighthouse right down just before the open sea. The cemetery must be somewhere between Queenscliff and that point. Drew had said he used to surf off the point – so beyond the lighthouse somewhere. And across the opening of the bay was Point Nepean.

Alex's geography was hazy, but he was surprised at how small the opening to Port Phillip Bay in fact was. So much water had to come in and out of that opening every tide. So much sea-going traffic.

He saw it all, the triangulation of The Rip – Queenscliff, Point Lonsdale, Point Nepean – the spots he had inhabited over the last couple of days. It felt like he was floating above and seeing the landscape through which he trudged or stumbled or was ferried, like a dotted line in an Indiana Jones movie. He felt comforted, somehow, with more of an idea of the landscape and his progress across it. More grounded perhaps.

This was welcome, because otherwise he wasn't feeling too grounded. There was the funeral, there was the drug cocktail of the other day, or series of days, but before that, long before that, he had been feeling uneasy. An itch. A wriggle in a too-tight collar.

It had been so good, so amazing, during the summer break. Everything between the three of them had been fine. But something was different now, he thought. He checked himself, though. No. Nothing was different. Nothing had changed, as such, about them, about the shape of their relationship, but it was as if something had moved around that shape, as if the sun had dropped further towards the horizon and the shadow the three of them threw across the ground had shifted, grown larger, perhaps, or become freakishly shaped.

It didn't feel the same between them. He certainly didn't feel the same about them. Well, he did feel precisely the same about Drew – even more hopelessly attached, if that could be possible. But Bec – he didn't feel the same about her. He felt wary of her. Alex supposed that partly it was seeing Drew and Bec together in Drew's family home. He hadn't realized Drew's family had met Bec before. He hadn't realized quite how much of a couple they looked, seemed, were, he supposed. But there, in that setting, he saw them as others must see them, the three of them that is – a fit young man, confident and charming, and a gorgeous smart young woman on his arm, with an easy smile and just as much charm – and him, the gay-best-friend, the gooseberry.

It wasn't like that. It had never been like that before. It didn't feel like that to him. Well, it hadn't. But in the simmer of that suburban family setting, things had been reduced, somehow, to a known common denominator, thickened like a careful béchamel sauce.

He didn't like how the other two played up to it. Drew, less so. He was just the same slack charmer as he always was, but adored, clearly, by his entire family. He was merely settling back into a comfortable old couch, the prince returned. Bec, though, she had played up to them. Alex had known her almost all his life and he knew when she had her game face on. Whether it was a half-marathon, an exam, wheedling a favour, or charming the potential in-laws – he had learned to see the determination underneath whatever was showing on the surface.

Alex pulled his chin in to his neck beneath the collar of Drew's coat. The shadows were shifting around his feet, tick-tocking smoothly from one hour to the next.

Everything was different. He couldn't deny it. Nothing had changed but everything was different. He didn't like it and he could do nothing about it. He gripped the railing, scanned the horizon and felt the weight of the canvas bag on his arm.

Ashley Sievwright is the author of *The Shallow End*, shortlisted in the Commonwealth Writers Prize 2009 for Best First Book; *Walter*; *Hothouse*, a novel published on Kindle; and the photographic books *A Year of Lighthouses*, and *Another Year of Lighthouses*. Ashley lives in Armadale, Melbourne.

Cut it Out

MANDY HENNINGHAM
TIFFANY JONES

Rethinking surgery on intersex infants

This year has seen intense debate in the media, parliament and policy back-rooms about surgical interventions on intersex infants. The potential to have intersex variations exists in all humans' prenatal development in the first few weeks – for a portion of humans a level of atypicality in sex traits continues on after this point (Ainsworth, 2015). Intersex variations are atypical sex characteristics; these can include chromosomes, genes, external genitalia, internal reproductive organs, hormones, or secondary characteristics (like body hair). In the last decade people with intersex variations have been increasingly studied or referred to as part of an umbrella group; rather than seen only as those with a specific variation such as for example Congenital Adrenal Hyperplasia (CAH) or Androgyn Insensitivity Syndromes (AIS). This group has also been termed (inappropriately) hermaphroditic, or as having 'disorders' of sex development (DSDs) – a large Australian survey showed the group preferred the person-centred 'term people with intersex variations' (Jones et al., 2016). Research has generally estimated that 1.7-4% of people are born intersex (OII Australia, 2012). Given some elements of sex (chromosomes, genes, hormones) are not apparent without testing, current estimates of the incidence and types of intersex variations may be conservative. The United Nations has recently affirmed the right to non-discrimination in healthcare for intersex youth, and has issued statements against early surgical interventions in the context of 'child torture' and 'LGBTI youth rights' broadly (Office of the High Commissioner for Human Rights, 2015; United Nations Human Rights Council, 2014). This chapter considers how health interventions for intersex youth have been recently studied in international research literature. It then compares these framings to the results of an international online survey of intersex people on their experiences of surgical intervention during their youth.

The Conflicted Literature on Surgery

Studies of the surgical interventions conducted on intersex youth in our review of the recent literature have featured a range of methods, including clinical and socially-oriented approaches. Participant numbers in these studies have ranged from sources with unclear numbers of intersex people (Dwyer, Ball, & Barker, 2015) through to sources with up to 272 participants (Jones, 2016). Most commonly the studies up until now have focussed on only one participant. Sources have also included a wide span of ages ranging from one day (Lucas-Herald, Rodie, Lucaccioni, Shapiro, & McNeilly, 2015) to 16-87 years of age (Jones, 2016); most commonly the studies used adults to consider youth healthcare retrospectively.

The two most common methods in recent studies are almost directly oppositional in their goals. Much of the recent literature for example used random medical case reports of individual patients' diagnosis and interventions (Bonanni, Pasetti, Ghiggeri, & Gandolfo, 2015; Ceci, Calleja, Said, & Gatt, 2015; Ekenze, Nwangwu, Amah, Agugua-obianyo, & Onuh, 2015; Latrech, Skikar, Mohammed El Hassan, Chraïbi, & Gaouzi, 2015; Mutlu, Kirmizibekmez, Aydin, Çetiner, & Moralioglu, 2015; Palanisamy, Patel, Sabnis, Palanisamy, & Vijay, 2015). These were pieces written by doctors or health academics on variably 1-108 intersex participants whom they had analysed and treated clinically – mainly just one infant or young person who had been subjected to tests (anatomical, hormonal, and/or radiological evaluations), and often hormonal and/or surgical interventions (e.g. genital surgeries such as gonad removals or cosmetic constructive work for example). Evaluations of the cases strongly privileged doctors' own positive assessment of their own clinical intervention's 'success' for the young intersex person. The sources largely did not report on the young participants' own assessment of their treatments.

The other particularly common method was autobiographical critical narratives – an individual intersex author's own critique of the intervention experiences in their youth or similar (Inter, 2015; Pagonis, 2015; Quinn, 2015; Simon, 2015; Truffer, 2015; Zieselman, 2015). These studies mainly considered the negative wellbeing impacts of intersex individuals receiving a lack of information during their youth and enduring often enforced interventions without their consent. The studies discuss their feelings of disconnection, trauma and depression, infertility, decreased sexual function/pleasure, undesired sex-based presentations, or surgical complications. A few studies similarly focussed on intersex participants' views on their own surgeries used a survey (Jones, 2016; Lin-Su, Lekarev, Poppas, & Vogiatzi, 2015; Wang & Tian, 2015). These studies considered teenagers through to significantly older adults' perspectives on their own experiences of quality of life, medical and social experiences. These studies problematized a range of health-care related issues including casting use of DSD as a disordering conceptualisation, noting problems with interventions and/or sexual experiences post-interventions, and decrying the lack of direct consultation around intersex peoples' needs in health-care (Wang & Tian, 2015), mental health (Lin-Su et al., 2015) and education (Jones, 2016).

Thus, the two main sets of literature provide wildly conflicting messages about health care intervention for intersex youth. On the one hand, literature from the medical research largely supports surgical interventions as generally 'successful' in achieving doctors' goals of correcting what they see as 'deformities'. On the other hand, literature from the sociological research and intersex individuals portrays surgical interventions as potentially problematic, harmful and often unwanted.

Clearly, there is a difference between the healthcare that is being provided to intersex youth and the healthcare that is wanted. There has therefore been a need to explore how healthcare for intersex youth could be improved.

An International Survey of People with Intersex Variations

Given that intersex people may view themselves or their identities in queer, psychiatric, medical or other terms (in their self-definition as intersex people, or someone with a disorder or variation for example), we wanted to create a study that was 'open' to diversity. We needed to avoid any tendency to absolutise differences between insiders and outsiders in intersex group memberships (Young, 1997). Therefore, we adopted a sociology of health in which each individual's view was treated as valid in its own right but acknowledged as largely incommensurable with the understandings of outsiders (Young, 1997). In many ways the project was organised around Critical research goals and methodologies: particularly casting 'intersex community guidance' on healthcare as primary above any external perspectives.

An anonymous Sydney University Medical School online survey was used to collect data from people with intersex variations, hosted by Survey Monkey. It was piloted by two intersex people first, to screen for inappropriate questions or insensitive wording and ensure it addressed the needs of the community. The survey questionnaire contained both forced-choice (quantitative) and open-ended (qualitative) questions. Data were obtained across eleven months (August 2014-June 2015). The recruitment process targeted participants with medically recognised intersex variations who were over the age of 18 and therefore able to reflect on their health care experiences during their 'whole youth' (infancy to adolescence). Processes included online advertisements and emails sent to clinics and health services, support organisation newsletters and online intersex networks on social media around the world (ensuring participation opportunities for a range of intersex people with different variations who had and had not experienced significant health interventions). Participants needed to self-select to join research. The survey was in English and covered health and other topics. Here we explore the data on demographics, diagnosis, early surgical intervention, physical and mental healthcare in youth, and the improvement of healthcare for youth. Descriptive and comparative statistical analyses were undertaken for the intersex participants' closed answer responses in SPSS, and grounded thematic analyses were prepared of their open answer written responses.

Results

Where Participants Came From

A total of 81 participants completed the survey, aged from 22 to 71yrs, with a mean age of 43yrs. Participants were born in 19 different countries; the largest portion of participants were born in the United States of America (n=38), followed by the United Kingdom (n=10), Canada (n=9) and Australia (n=8). These four countries particularly had active intersex community networks supporting the survey's promotion. Participants had an array of educational backgrounds, with 35% completing tertiary education and 27% completing postgraduate studies. A further 14% stated they had completed some tertiary education and another 14% completing a trade certificate. Only 10% had halted their education after completing high school. This suggested a lower dropout rate overall than in an earlier Australia-only study; which found 18% of 272 intersex people had not completed high-school due to complications from early surgical intervention (Jones, 2016).

Region of Birth	No. of participants
North America	47
Europe	20
Asia-Pacific	12
Africa	1
Total	80

Figure 1: Participants' region of birth.

The majority of participants were assigned female at birth (54%), fewer were assigned male (39%). The remaining participants were assigned one sex and then reassigned another during their infancy, or were not assigned a sex. Overall, most of the participants (52%) currently identified as women, a smaller portion identified as men (17%), some were gender fluid (5%), genderless (4%) and the remainder had a combination of identities. This reflected findings in an Australian study that those assigned male at birth were more likely to have a different gender identity later in life (Jones et al., 2016). In total, almost a third of participants had identities that challenged the two gender binary norms and identified as either fluid or their own subjective interpretation of gender. For example one participant said, 'If I could become third gender, a hermaphrodite I would. I was born to be both and I want my body to be both'.

When Intersex Variations Were Diagnosed

Participants received a range of diagnoses for their intersex variations. Androgyn insensitivities/AIS were the most common diagnoses (25%), followed by Ambiguous Genitalia (15%), Congenital Adrenal Hyperplasia/CAH (12%), Klinefelter's Syndrome (8%), Ovotesticular conditions (6%), Mosaicism (6%), Hypospadias (5%), 46XXY (5%), Gonadal Dysgenesis (3%) and 47XXY (3%). Other reported variations included Progestin Induced Viralisation/PIV, Mayer-Rokitansky-Küster-Hauser/MKRH and Swyer's Syndrome. For most participants, diagnosis occurred during their youth. Specifically, 34% were diagnosed 0-3yrs; 9% were aged 4-10yrs; and 13% were 11-17yrs. Only 13% were 18-25yrs, and 32% were 25+yrs. Most (60%) reported that they did not feel like they were fully informed about their intersex variation during their youth, and many expressed a desire for earlier information in their comments. One participant explained, 'I wish I had been diagnosed as a child, it would have allowed me to be at one with the person I now am'.

Surgical Intervention During Youth

A total of 60% of participants received surgery during infancy or childhood, 37% did not, the remainder were unsure. Importantly, most (64%) of those aged under 40yrs had received surgical intervention in infancy or childhood; suggesting that this was not a declining practice in the last half century. A strong majority of 96% of participants stated that they felt the surgery was inappropriate; only a few individuals felt that the surgery was appropriate. Participants were asked in a write-in question whether upon reflection as an adult, *'you wish you had received surgical intervention as an infant?'* The majority (over three quarters) just said 'no' or answered in the negative with minimal comment. A further eight participants stated that infants could not consent to such a procedure; for example a participant clarified, 'The fact I was a child undergoing such treatment created a real sense of difference and was completely dis-empowering to me because I could not consent to it'. Another participant explained, 'Some of the surgery could have waited until I was old enough to understand and consent. I may have agreed to the surgery, but I would have preferred it to happen with my consent'. Only two participants wished they did receive surgical intervention earlier; one to 'better prepare' for adulthood; the other 'for health purposes'.

Attitudes Towards Physical Healthcare

Participants were asked if they had *'sufficient healthcare management regarding your intersex variation?'*. Four fifths of the group did not; only one fifth had sufficient healthcare. Many who experienced insufficient healthcare discussed how they did not receive enough support, had health professionals with no training in intersex issues, did not feel their intersex status was distinguished from being transgender, or experienced limited handover in their healthcare from adolescence to adulthood. Typical participant comments included 'no access to (intersex) specialists, and no ongoing support' and, 'I have never had proper care'. Lack of training for healthcare professionals often resulted in participants being misgendered or referred to with mixed gendered terminology; one participant said their physician would often contradict herself by 'using 'clitoris' in one sentence and 'phallus' in the next, which becomes offensive and invalidating' – and confusing to a child. Only two participants mentioned that their care was limited due to their area of residence; the primary issue appeared to be lack of supports for 'intersex youth' generally. These findings reflected other studies showing intersex people believe a lack of training for health care professionals is a major issue (Davis, 2015; Jones, 2016).

Participants who received sufficient healthcare mainly explained that it involved having a doctor who was able to manage an array of medical complications, or multiple health professionals who were educated in different intersex health concerns. Three participants discussed having access to multiple health services which allowed their variation to be treated as a complex issue. One of these participants had both 'a very good reproductive endocrinologist' and 'an excellent therapist about facing my CAIS diagnosis'. The participants also talked about the value of self-directed care; taking ownership over their own bodies (self-determination) and educating themselves on their own variations and then finding doctors that suited them. One of the participants explained, 'I am in charge and empowered in my healthcare. Big difference: I am educated about my CAIS. I ask lots of questions, unlike my parents'. They also mentioned seeking out intersex support groups as part of their care, 'Knew nothing as a child but AISSG group (...) enlightened me'. This showed that poor healthcare could not only be turned around by training, but by empowerment of intersex youth through their exposure to alternate intersex-run information sources.

Attitudes Towards Mental Health Support

The majority of 75% of participants reported seeking mental health support. The participants' comments suggested three clear mental health support seeking trends: seeking gender counselling, seeking counselling for mental health issues (depression, suicidal thoughts), and seeking counselling for PTSD surrounding their health interventions.

However, a write-in comment question on the quality of mental health support experiences showed that of those who did seek mental health support, only 15% had a positive experience. There was little difference between those allocated female or male sex markers in terms of seeking mental health support as adults or mental health support quality, and no difference by region. Negative experiences in seeking mental health services were mainly explained as difficulties in finding appropriate mental health supports (that they did not exist for intersex youth), or existing services being unhelpful. A typical comment included, 'did go to therapy for a while but then that therapist moved to another place (…) It didn't help me much anyway'.

Mental health professionals' lack of education on intersex issues was also frustrating for many participants. One commented that they had to educate therapists; who generally 'have heard the word intersex, but that is about it'. Some participants had bad experiences. For example, one participant commented that their therapist tried to make them more masculine, and that 'The experience was terrible and the therapist refused to acknowledge my bisexuality (…) I quit'. Another stated, 'They [mental health professionals] ignored my childhood medical history, and would not let me talk about the gender assignment issues'. Of the participants who sought the support of a mental health service and reported having a positive experience, written descriptive responses ranged from it being 'adequate' to statements such as 'I would not have survived suicidal depression without mental health support'.

Improving Healthcare Overall

Participants were asked how they felt the management and support of intersex children could be improved. Out of 66 written responses, one of the most strongly recommended areas for improvement was healthcare professional training (23 participants). A participant commented for example that healthcare professionals needed to learn, 'validation of gender and use of properly gendered words and terminology that affirms the person's identity'. Another commented that health professionals needed to, 'recognize that variation in biologic sex is normal and not a problem that needs to be fixed'. Equally, another strong message was the call to delay medical and surgical intervention until an age of consent (23 participants). One participant explained, 'listen to the person no matter how old they are. Don't give meds or do surgery unless the person has agreed it's a good idea' (at an appropriate age).

A further 13 participants discussed a need for greater mental health support and access, and another 13 participants desired more resources about intersex variations. Seven participants discussed a need for peer support groups for intersex youth or parents, and five suggested better long-term support and follow ups. Some individual comments reflected on the need to prevent hurtful experiences; one comment specifically discussed the problem of children being ridiculed, 'Be honest with children, they are not stupid. I was put down by a doctor who made fun of my hypogonadism and penis size'.

The Need to Delay Surgical Intervention

Overall the international survey data reflected the strong incidence of surgical intervention for intersex people seen in country-specific large-scale surveys, case studies and autobiographical literature from around the world. In the literature review, most medical studies promoted interventionist perspectives pathologising 'patients with DSDs' and propounding the need for surgical interventions. Contrastingly, the survey data reported in this article showed that although early 'corrective' surgical intervention was widespread, it was largely unwanted. Almost all participants felt the surgery they experienced was inappropriate, and three quarters would not wish for surgery in infancy or childhood. This finding reinforced the individual stories of regret around interventions and resistance to interventionist approaches found in the narratives of intersex individuals (Baratz & Karkazis, 2015; Cynthia, 2015; Pagonis, 2015).

The study showed that the disordering medical literature is misconceived. A pro-active stance towards aligning the range of perspectives on health-care for intersex people needs to be taken by a range of stakeholders (from policy-makers to health-care providers) if the tensions between intersex people and healthcare professionals are to be resolved. Anti-discrimination legislation at the international level needs to be drawn upon where possible to justify the need for non-discriminatory revisions to current approaches delaying surgical and other interventions and only allowing them in the event of the patient's informed consent, as is starting to happen in Australia and Malta (Jones et al., 2016). The data on good healthcare experiences in the study implied poor healthcare could not only be turned around by training as argued elsewhere (Davis, 2015) but also by empowerment of intersex youth through their exposure to alternate information sources. Community supports for intersex youth therefore need to be developed and funded in a range of contexts, and may conceivably be enhanced through targeted UNESCO and other civil society campaigns. It is time to cut out unnecessary early surgical intervention on intersex infants around the world.

References

Ainsworth, C. (2015). Sex Redefined. *Nature, 518*(1), 288-291.

Baratz, A., & Karkazis, K. (2015). Cris de Coeur and the Moral Imperative to Listen to and Learn from Intersex People. *Narrative Inquiry in Bioethics, 5*(2), 127-132.

Bonanni, A., Pasetti, F., Ghiggeri, G. M., & Gandolfo, C. (2015). Renal denervation for severe hypertension in a small child with Turner syndrome: miniaturisation of the procedure and results. *BMJ Case Reports, 2015*(1), 1-5.

Ceci, M., Calleja, E., Said, E., & Gatt, N. (2015). A Case of True Hermaphroditism Presenting as a Testicular Tumour. *Case Reports in Urology, 1*(1), 1.

Cynthia, A. (2015). Navigating Intersex Healthcare: My Odyssey. *Narrative Inquiry in Bioethics, 5*(2), E3-E5.

Davis, G. (2015). *Contesting Intersex: The Dubious Diagnosis*. New york: NYU Press.

Dwyer, A., Ball, M., & Barker, E. (2015). Policing LGBTIQ people in rural spaces: emerging issues and future concerns. *Rural Society, 24*(3), 227-243.

Ekenze, S., Nwangwu, E., Amah, C., Agugua-obianyo, N., & Onuh, A. (2015). Disorders of sex development in a developing country. *Pediatric Surgery International, 31*(1), 93-99.

Inter, L. (2015). Finding My Compass. *Narrative Inquiry in Bioethics, 5*(2), 95-98.

Jones, T. (2016). The Needs of Students with Intersex Variations. *Sex Education, 16*(6), 602-618. Retrieved from http://www.tandfonline.com/doi/abs/10.1080/14681811.2016.114980 8?journalCode=csed20

Jones, T., Hart, B., Carpenter, M., Ansara, G., Leonard, W., & Lucke, J. (2016). *Intersex: Stories and Statistics from Australia.* London: Open Book Publisher.

Latrech, H., Skikar, I., Mohammed El Hassan, G., Chraïbi, A., & Gaouzi, A. (2015). Disorder of Sexual Development and Congenital Heart Defect in 47XYY: Clinical Disorder or Coincidence? *Case Reports in Endocrinology, 802162*(1), 1-5.

Lin-Su, K., Lekarev, O., Poppas, D. P., & Vogiatzi, M. G. (2015). Congenital adrenal hyperplasia patient perception of 'disorders of sex development nomenclature. *International Journal of Pediatric Endocrinology, 2015*(9), 1.

Lucas-Herald, A. K., Rodie, M., Lucaccioni, L., Shapiro, D., & McNeilly, J. (2015). The pitfalls associated with urinary steroid metabolite ratios in children undergoing investigations for suspected disorders of steroid synthesis. *International Journal of Pediatric Endocrinology, 2015*(9), 1.

Mutlu, G. Y., Kirmizibekmez, H., Aydin, H., Çetiner, H., & Moralioglu, S. (2015). Pure gonadal dysgenesis (Swyer syndrome) due to microdeletion in the SRY gene. *Journal of Pediatric Endocrinology & Metabolism, 28*(1-2), 207-210.

Office of the High Commissioner for Human Rights. (2015). Intersex Fact Sheet. Geneva: United Nations.

OII Australia. (2012). *Intersex for allies.* Retrieved from Melbourne: http://oii.org.au/21336/intersex-for-allies/

Pagonis, P. (2015). The Son They Never Had. *Narrative Inquiry in Bioethics, 5*(2), 103-106.

Palanisamy, S., Patel, N., Sabnis, S., Palanisamy, N., & Vijay, A. (2015). Laparoscopic hysterectomy with bilateral orchidectomy for Persistent Mullerian duct syndrome with seminoma testes: Case report. *Journal of Minimal Access Surgery, 11*(4).

Quinn, E. (2015). Standing Up. *Narrative Inquiry in Bioethics, 5*(2), 109-111.

Simon, L. (2015). XY/XO. *Narrative Inquiry in Bioethics, 5*(2), E11-E14.

Truffer, D. (2015). It's a Human Rights Issue! *Narrative Inquiry in Bioethics, 5*(2), 111-114.

A/HRC/RES/27/32 Human rights, sexual orientation and gender identity, (2014).

Wang, C., & Tian, Q. (2015). The Investigation of Quality of Life in 87 Chinese Patients with Disorders of Sex Development. *BioMed Research International, 2015*(342420), 1-6.

Young, R. (1997). Comparative Methodology and Postmodern Relativism. *International Review of Education, 43*(5), 497-505.

Zieselman, K. (2015). Invisible Harm. *Narrative Inquiry in Bioethics, 5*(2), 122-125.

_____

Mandy Henningham studies at the Discipline of Child and Adolescent Health, Sydney Medical School at the University of Sydney. She completed her Master of Health Science (Sexual Health) at the Health Science campus at the University of Sydney. Through this degree, she found her passion to pursue LGBTI and human rights. Mandy pursued other degrees in health such as a Graduate Certificate in Public Health and also completed a Bachelor of Health and Movement (Sport) which fuelled her passion for health and fitness. This background in health as well has led Mandy to pursue research interests in LGBTIQ health.

Tiffany Jones (PhD) researches LGBTI issues, sociology of education and health, and policy at Macquarie University. She is an adjunct Associate Professor at La Trobe University. Her projects have been funded by the ARC, UNESCO, beyondblue and others. She authored *Intersex: Stories and Statistics* and other titles. She has liaised with the UN, UNESCO and government and non-government organisations. She sits on the editorial board of *LGBT Health* and *LGBT Youth*, and edits *Bent Street*. She received the Griffith University Medal, Association for Women Educators Award for Girls' Education, and ATLAS International Institute for Qualitative Methodology Highly Commended Dissertation Award.

Flowers | GUY JAMES WHITWORTH

Interview

_____

DENNIS ALTMAN

GORDON THOMPSON, *BENT STREET* PUBLISHER, INTERVIEWS DENNIS ALTMAN

GORDON THOMPSON: I'm with Dennis Altman discussing 2017. It's not exactly the year in review, because we are talking in late October and the declaration of the same sex marriage postal survey and so much else lies ahead, but let me start by asking, how has your year gone – so far?

DENNIS ALTMAN: When you say 'your' year do you mean my year personally, or do you mean how do I see the year?

GT: A bit of both.

DA: We are almost exactly a year from the moment when Donald Trump was elected. And I was in California the week of the election, which was a quite remarkable time, because California of course was very heavily anti-Trump. And I start there because I think we've all been, in a sense, in the shadow of Trump over the last year. And while I think it's really important to say we're in Australia, he is not our President, there's a way in which a triumph of a certain sort of right-wing populism seems to be forbidding in many parts of the world. We're talking the day after the Czechs have just elected a right-wing populist government and I think that sort of a background is necessary as we think about what's going on globally and what's going on in the larger political world, not just what's going on in the queer world.

If we talk about the queer world, the last couple of weeks have been quite extraordinary. I've felt a huge amount of energy. I think that the marriage campaign has created a whole new generation of activists and a huge sense of community, that is much bigger than people anticipated, but I'm also speaking just as the Melbourne Festival has ended and what was very interesting was the centrepiece of the Festival, Taylor Mac's extraordinary 24-hour performance of America in Song. Which was a very, very queer event. So there's been this real sense of queer community and queer culture over the last couple of months. I'm using Taylor Mac and Trump as interestingly both American, but as polar opposites of the sort of ways in which the world is going.

GT: And how is the world going?

DA: I think this has been a very bad year for queer rights globally. There have been some very unpleasant developments and in fact in Melbourne back in May there was a demonstration around Chechnya, but what went on in Chechnya is probably no worse than what is now happening in other parts of Central Asia, in Egypt. There are some very worrying developments going on in Indonesia. I think that what is happening is – and it's something that I wrote about last year in a book with my colleague John Symons called *Queer Wars*, about the way in which global polarisation around queer rights is becoming quite central – and while things are clearly getting much better in countries like Australia that's, unfortunately, not the case in the majority of parts of the world.

GT: Do you think the advent of Trump gave permission for a lot more of this, or was this coming from a long time ago?

DA: No, I don't think this has anything really to do with Trump. It has to do with Trump in the sense that the US was very active in using its diplomatic and financial resources to support LGBT groups in various parts of the world, and that certainly has declined considerably. But the impetus certainly goes back way before Trump, and it comes from a whole set of religious and political authoritarian leaders who find homosexuality a very useful way of rallying support, often in defending the nation and culture against Western imperialism. Having a President of the United States who seems to share some of their views might, in a very odd way, mitigate some of the polarisation. Not I think in a particular productive way. But this is not something that has begun this year, or that we can connect directly to changes in the US.

GT: So in terms of mitigating the abuse of rights, what might be some of the solutions? For instance, if same sex marriage in Australia is galvanising the community as you say, is that then a way forward, or a model?

DA: I don't think it's a model for the rest of the world. I think that the enormous emphasis on marriage has been very counterproductive in many parts of the world. The idea that if you acknowledge any sort of sexual diversity, this leads to same-sex marriage and the destruction of the traditional family, is exactly what people like Putin, a lot of leaders across Africa and the Middle East are saying. In fact, one has to be very very careful about assuming that what might be the goals of a movement in a rich Western liberal country are transferrable elsewhere. I think we have to talk about what's happening here remembering that what's happening here is not replicable in other parts of the world. But certainly, there is a great deal that can be done in terms of giving quiet support to people. The most essential thing that can be done is recognising that increasing numbers of people are fleeing their countries because they are being persecuted for their sexuality. Australia could be much more active and much more overt in saying we will accept people who are refugees because of their sexuality. This applies immediately and horrifically to some of the people who are currently being held offshore in PNG and Nauru.

GT: In *The Guardian* (Australian edition, 9 October 2017) you wrote about how activism in the community has been invigorated because of the survey, but what might be some of the other effects?

DA: The immediate effect is that, because of the poll, people went and enrolled to vote who might otherwise not have enrolled, and this is likely to boomerang back on the government that instituted the poll. And if you look at where the greatest enrolments took place it seems to be in inner-city electorates, and there are not that many government seats this puts in peril, but it will possibly have some impact on the next election. But more importantly I think people have discovered the possibility of being politically active. A lot of people have been out there doorknocking, making telephone calls, and demonstrating in the streets.

...I think people have discovered the possibility of being politically active. A lot of people have been out there doorknocking, making telephone calls, and demonstrating ...

I think it's an open question what happens to that after November. Do they all say, if it's a 'yes' vote, that yes, we won and disappear, or does this mean there is a new group of people who have been energised by an initiation into political activity who then take that further. I, of course, would like to believe that's the case, but I might be being overly optimistic.

GT: The current debate, is it changing the parties in any way?

DA: I don't think so. I think that the Labor party has clearly moved to a position where almost everybody in the Labor party has become a strong supporter of the community, and often it's quite genuine. I can certainly recognise that there are political advantages in this and there are certainly strategic questions about competing with the Greens in the inner city, but it is quite genuine, certainly on the part of Bill Shorten, whom I've talked to. Bill's much more enthusiastic about same sex marriage than I am.

The Liberal party – it's been interesting – when the small number of Liberals tried to get a free vote in the parliament they got nowhere and this is quite fascinating given that the Liberal party has always said they believe, unlike Labor, in not binding their MPs. I think the degree of hypocrisy that now exists within the federal Liberal party is quite unparalleled since Menzies set up that party. There is something so bizarre about a party that keeps saying they stand for parliamentary democracy and the Westminster tradition, the independence of MPs – taking no notice of any of these beliefs. It will be interesting to see how the Liberal Party deals with the results of the poll, because, problem is, *we're* having this discussion *before* the results, but you will publish *after* the results …

GT: And what about the minor parties, such as the Nationals, and the independents?

DA: The Greens have, of course, always been very strongly supportive of same sex marriage. And I think the Greens feel a bit pissed off because they feel that people have forgotten their leadership in that. I don't think beyond that … look, one of the things one has to remember is that for most people it's not a huge issue, and it's difficult to remember that because we're talking about this in the middle of a campaign that is getting a lot of media attention, and we're talking about it for a queer audience. But there are an awful lot of people out there who really aren't that interested. I think that the fact that we're going to get something like a 70% return in the postal survey is quite amazing. And far from being bothered by the fact that there are millions of people who haven't sent back their votes, I think its extraordinary that already more have sent back their votes than turn out to vote in elections in most democratic countries.

GT: We've heard from overseas campaigners that 'we've had same sex marriage for a few years now and the sky hasn't fallen in'. But obviously some things will change. If same sex marriage is introduced in this country, what do you think will be the changes to queer identity, or indeed, what will happen to marriage?

DA: I don't see why it should have major changes. Both the 'yes' and the 'no' cases for their own reasons have made this seem much more important than it is. I think all this argument that somehow if we bring in marriage there will be a reduction in people committing suicide is probably wrong. I think that if there were a 'no' vote, that would have a really bad effect on people's mental health. A 'no' vote would be read by a lot of people who are already feeling that they're marginalised, victimised as confirmation. I think a 'no' vote would certainly underscore that, so a 'no' vote would be very dangerous.

_____

For me the issue is not so much the right to get married but the right not to get married: to have the right to say I'm not interested in marriage.

_____

But if same sex marriage comes in, a lot of couples will get married in the first six months and after that it will just become part of the normal pattern of life. Marriage clearly is changing, lots of couples don't choose to get married, an awful lot of marriages break up. For me the issue is not so much the right to get married but the right not to get married: to have the right to say I'm not interested in marriage. And I think there is a danger in the marriage argument, which is that it too easily holds that up as the only way that people can live a life. Often, people who are not in long-lasting stable relationships can be made to feel failures. So I think that the hyperbole of the marriage campaign can be quite dangerous – not in quite the same way as the hyperbole of the 'no' case, but it still has to be recognised that any campaign in which people are forced to take exaggerated positions, which a popular plebiscite forces, has dangers.

GT: With what we're talking about – Trump, activism, community – it seems that social media is now a major factor in creating opinion and inflaming situations …

DA: We know that extraordinary untruths get passed very quickly through social media. During the American campaign there were all these absolutely extraordinary claims such as the Pope has endorsed Trump. Hilary Clinton is dying of whatever nasty disease was the choice of that week. And those sorts of total fabrications get constantly repeated and the alt-right in the US were very clever in their use of social media and the other side of it is that social media works in ways that we tend to constantly be reinforced in what we believe and we see that reflected in mainstream media. The Murdoch press in general makes no pretence any longer of objective journalism. If you look at the way they run their stories and their headlines they've given up the idea that used to be sacred if you were running a newspaper: that you tried to be objective, you tried to make a real distinction between reporting and commentary. To some extent the Fairfax press on the other side is now doing this as well. I think that's very sad, so even in the mainstream press we see some of those aspects that are constantly attributed to social media.

The other side, of course, is that social media does mean that people can be connected to each other in ways that were impossible until we had Facebook and Google and the rest of them. The world has changed so quickly, we are so used to being constantly connected to everybody all the time – I mean, you and I are sitting here recording a voice memo on a mobile phone. Even twenty years ago that would have seemed slightly science-fiction-y. The thing about the current ways of communication is that it makes us more parochial and more global. I mean, we're more global because we have access to things you once had to go to a library for. Now you can just go online, you can read newspapers, you can look at TV and do all that stuff from anywhere in the world. On the other hand it makes us more parochial, because most of us most of the time stay in our bubble and our prejudices and biases are constantly reinforced.

GT: What are the books, or the writers, this year, that have struck you as significant – what are the new voices in the area?

DA: That's a very good question. The books that come to mind that I've read recently, none of them are queer, I mean the ones that strike me as significant. I think there are some new voices coming out around issues that my generation dealt with in very different ways and I think very inadequately, and that is particularly around trans issues, and there is a whole growing articulation of trans positions. I can't think of any particular individual work, I haven't for example read Eddy Ayres' new autobiography, but I used to listen to him when he was Emma Ayres a ABC Classic FM broadcaster, but that whole area, which is shaking up all sorts of assumptions about gender, has probably been one of the biggest themes of the last couple of years.

I am somewhat depressed by how little interest queer activists have in reading; how little understanding there is of the importance of reading fiction.

I think there are some very interesting books from outside Australia, there is an emerging literature from many parts of the world where being queer is highly stigmatised, highly victimised. There's no individual title that comes to mind, but I think that what I'd say is that I am somewhat depressed by how little interest queer activists have in reading; how little understanding there is of the importance of reading fiction. I'm constantly struck by the fact that every time I get to do something, people want to introduce me as an activist, but I say, no, I'm a writer, I'm not an activist. And somehow that doesn't have the same clout. I think that's unfortunate. I'm also struck by the fact that if you make literary references, not many people get them. I was in Ballarat for the writer's festival and went through a whole explanation of why I wanted to be called a writer and not an activist. I said that writing requires you to see ambiguities and nuances and contradictions, and activism doesn't work that way.

GT: Well, with the *Speak Now* collection, which we published six years ago, basically it was 'yes', 'no' and 'ambivalent' opinions and reflections on same-sex marriage. But it didn't set the world on fire, and I wonder if that's because it had that ambivalence.

DA: Oh, I don't think it's because of that; books just don't. Collections like that very rarely do, to be honest. I think that single author polemics do.

GT: So, there's a marketing lesson there ...

DA: That's right. I also think it's true that books do not influence people in the way they used to. Some of course can, but, by and large, I'm struck by how little reference there is to books by people who are in movements. And also, as movements become bigger and more organised, they become very referential and people do read, but they read reports, then they read each other's reports and they don't understand about reading fiction at all. So I'm quite pessimistic about that ...

GT: One last quick question. Why do you get up in the morning?

DA: ... Well, what else do you do?

––––––––––––––––

Dennis Altman is a Professorial Fellow in the Institute for Human Security at LaTrobe University. He has written over a dozen books including *Queer Wars*. He was President of the AIDS Society of Asia and the Pacific (2001-5), and Board member of the Governing Council of the International AIDS Society and Oxfam Australia. He was listed by *The Bulletin* as one of the 100 most influential Australians ever, and is a Member of the Order of Australia 2008. In 2013 he was awarded the American Sociological Association Simon and Gagnon Award for career contributions to sociology of sexualities.

Cultural Mobility

STEVE R. E. PEREIRA

I seem to have one of those odd physiognomies that defy easy cultural identification. I am of Indian extraction; my family originates from Goa; and though I was born and raised in Tanzania, we are now three generations down dispersed across several continents. I have the round face, bulbous nose, thick, kinky mop of hair (when I had any) of my South Indian antecedents. Not so usual though, but not uncommon in South Indians, is that my skin tone tends to fairness, what colour-conscious Indians approvingly call *'wheatish'* – a milky coffee. I do however tan to a dark brown in the sun.

Given that I think I have a quite specific South Indianess to my features I am always rather surprised that I am so often mistaken for a person from other cultures.

 C3

Years ago, while I was living in Canada, I went back to Goa to attend a family wedding. I was flying out of Goa to Bombay when our flight was inexplicably cancelled and we were put up for the night in a hotel that I would not have otherwise been able to afford. That evening in the dining room I looked up from my solitary place at a solitary table and saw an ostentatiously well-dressed, smooth-skinned and pomaded, plumpish, youngish (my age at the time, the mid-twenties) Middle Eastern-looking man staring at me. He was seated at a table with another man of similar age, but of very different appearance. The other man was leaner, swarthier, and bearded, but was dressed in similar clothing to the first man that was both too short and too large for him. Hand-me-downs from the first man is what it looked like to me. By the time I had finished my observation, I had realised that they were both staring at me. Disconcerted, I smiled a noncommittal smile and went back to my book and coffee. A few minutes later I heard a rustle and looked up. The second man was at my table, the first one looking on from his. I looked at the man. Smiled.

He didn't smile back. He said something to me in Arabic. I said, 'I don't speak Arabic.' He looked surprised. 'You are not Kuwaiti?' he said in heavily accented English. I shook my head, 'No I am not. I am an Indian. From Goa, here. But I live in Canada.' A moment of silence then he said: 'We thought you were Kuwaiti.' I looked at him and then at the other man still seated at his table who was staring at me, fork full of cake suspended halfway to his open mouth. 'Are you Kuwaiti?' I asked. He shook his head no. 'Qatar,' he said. I nodded. Pause. I inclined my head towards the other man. 'Is that your friend?' placing just a bit more emphasis on *friend* to make it sound like something else, but not quite. He looked back at the man and then at me. 'Boss,' he said. 'He is my boss.' 'Ok, I said.' He stood at my table for a moment more then went back to his without another word.

As he sat down, I could see him shake his head at the other man and say 'India' then shrug and say 'Canada'. He gestured upwards with both open palms to suggest he was confused. They both turned to look at me. I smiled, shrugged my shoulders and went back to my book which I couldn't read anymore.

Five minutes later I decide to leave. As I am getting my stuff together, I glance across at their table. They are both staring at me. I look away. But I have to pass their table on the way to the door. My strategy is to approach, look at them, half smile, look away, exit. But I time the look too late and catch the first man's eye just as I am close enough for him to say to me, 'Do you want to come to my room to dance?' I stop. 'Sure,' I say immediately and instinctively. 'No' would have required an explanation, and I had none to offer.

The three of us head up the stairs to the second floor. I'm not inclined to make any more conversation and neither, it seems, are they. We arrive at a large suite overlooking the expansive pool and with panoramic views of the ocean. Man One, the Boss, we still haven't exchanged names, disappears into the bedroom. Man Two fiddles with a humongous ghetto blaster (this was the early 1990s). Was this in their carry-on luggage? I walk over and admire the view which is admirable. When the thump of a disco mix fills the room, Man One comes back. He has changed from a purple Lacoste polo top, sky blue Ralph Lauren madras checked shorts and purple Salvatore Ferragamo python-skin loafers to leather-look short shorts, a metallic mesh knit tank top, thick socks and yellow suede construction boots. International Male active wear is my not-uneducated guess. He starts gyrating to the music. Man Two joins in. They are both surprisingly smooth, unselfconscious, movers. They are self-contained. They aren't dancing with each other. Neither of them says a word, nor do I. When Nomad's 'Devotion' comes on about three songs in I start dancing too. We are all dancing. We are not dancing with each other. I dance to my reflection in the glass, watch the sun set and fret about returning to Canada. We dance for the next two hours without saying anything to each other.

Just before midnight I head to the door and wave good night to them. They wave back and use that as a way to segue into *bhangra* moves. I get myself to my room and bed. I fly out the next morning for Bombay.

CB

I was in Havana in 1994 and was walking around town with Heinz, a German tourist who was staying at the same hotel and with whom I had joined up for an excursion into the city, because I was travelling alone and his wife was not feeling well. We were just wandering around killing time before we had to catch a bus back to the resort at Varadero when this tough-looking, complete with tats and scowl, Cuban guy approached us.

I recognised him with some alarm. He had eyed me off at a bar the night before. He had looked out of place there in a crowd of primed and preening queens and had been hard to miss. He had mistaken my look of curiosity for interest, and it had been difficult to shake him off. But eventually, I did and had forgotten all about him until now. And here he was. He was glaring at me. He ignored Heinz but grabbed me by the arm and said something rapidly in Spanish. I looked at him, looked at Heinz, who did speak a bit of Spanish, but who now just looked confused. I said to the Cuban guy in English, 'I don't speak Spanish.' He looked surprised and then he went back to looking ferocious. He was still holding my arm by the bicep hard. He sucked on his teeth noisily, jerked his head dismissively at Heinz and whispered sibilantly in my ear, 'Estás Cubana. Don't forget your heritage!' He let my arm go and then walked off without a look back. I looked at Heinz who just shrugged and said, 'He thought you were Cuban.' I just nodded at him then, but a few moments later when we had resumed walking, I said with an ever-so-slight laugh, 'I think he thought you were my lover.' Heinz stopped short and looked at me in what looked like horror. 'But how is that possible?' he said. No, not said, exclaimed! Loudly. He seemed really bothered. I wasn't sure whether he was questioning the possibility of us being perceived as lovers; or the possibility of us being actual lovers; or the possibility that he of all people could be perceived as gay. So, I just widened my eyes at him and walked on. He never quite caught up with me, and we sat on the bus together but apart.

Later I recounted the story to his wife when we met at the pool. She looked at me intently and said, a deep frown furrowing her brow, 'But Heinz is not homosexual.' She seemed really, really bothered. I wasn't sure by what exactly. I said nothing, again, but must have looked something. A beat of silence, and then she shot a look at me like an accusation of some sort. I belly flopped into the pool. It hurt. We stayed away from each other for the rest of the trip.

℘

Almost exactly a year later I was in Melbourne, walking down La Trobe Street in the middle of the city when I lock glances with three Indigenous youths walking towards me. When we catch up to each other, we involuntarily pause.

'Where are you from bro?' said one.

'Yeah,' said the other. 'Where are you from?'

They were friendly, but there was, or did I assume, an edge of aggression in their tone. I didn't know how to respond. I don't know how to respond at the best of times to where-are-you-from questions. Where do I say – Canada, Tanzania, India, Goa? I just say India, which is what I think I am most identifiably. So I said India. They looked at me in disbelief.

'You're a fucking Indian?'

I nod, seems safest. They laugh uproariously. One steps right up to me, right up. I can smell mint and bubblegum on his breath, feel the heat of his body. 'You're a bro, bro,' he says clapping me on the shoulder. Then each of the others reach out and touch my hand, my arm. One winks at me with a very cheeky and yes, sexy grin.

I say, 'Thank you,' and watch them walk away still laughing. Catching a reflection of myself in a shop window, I realise I am smiling. The city feels less alien. For a while.

ᴄʒ

At University earlier this year I get lost looking for my supervisor's office and end up in some sort of common room. There is a young man there. Quite beautiful in a classic British, Merchant-Ivory kind of way; all peaches and cream, foppish blond hair, oh-so-aquiline nose and strawberry lips. Not my type, but stare-worthy nonetheless. He notes my interest and rises with a smile. Over the course of a ten-minute conversation that is arguably mutually flirtatious, he tells me with great enthusiasm about his research project, which has to do with indigenous music and sounds fascinating. But about half-way through, something in the way he looks at me, his phrasing, his tone, makes me think that he thinks I am indigenous myself. I let him go on for a while, but then can't help myself and interrupt saying, 'I get the impression you think I'm indigenous.' He stops short and blinks at me, but says nothing. 'I'm not indigenous,' I say, 'I'm actually Indian.' He still says nothing, so I add, 'I get mistaken for being indigenous a lot, even by indigenous people.' His look is grim. If he wasn't so willowy, and I twice his size, I would think he wanted to hit me. 'You know,' he finally spits out, 'that is a form of cultural appropriation. It's fucking cultural appropriation.' He jabs his finger at me. 'Mate.' Final finger jab and then he stalks off.

∞

At a literary festival in Williamstown an elderly (white) woman, came up to me at a book table I was staffing. It was a quiet moment and we had a lovely chat about her life in Yorkshire and how her daughter loved living in Australia, and it wasn't like anything she had been told to expect and that the country and land and people were so wonderful and how really progressive the country was that she could have a conversation with me at a literary festival. When her daughter came to collect her, she said goodbye, but then turned around and told me in somewhat of a whisper that 'I was a credit to my community'. I said, 'Thank you.' I had no idea of which community she was talking about, or what else to say. She meant well.

∞

Not so laudatory was a large group of (white) Australian 'grey nomads' at a hotel campsite in Central Australia. When I, very dark from ten days of camping in the unforgiving sun, dressed in shorts and thongs, very sweaty and very dusty after a long trek, entered the communal kitchen to fill a kettle for a much needed cup of tea. The group who were sitting around in a large circle reacted in shock. They literally tried to shoo me away with 'shoo' noises and 'go away' gestures, as you would a recalcitrant goat. No invitation to dance here. I, more bemused than anything, re-checked that I had read the 'communal kitchen' sign correctly and then looked at them blankly. I may have said, 'What?' I'm not entirely sure.

One of the women said slowly and emphatically, 'The grounds are reserved for guests only.' Then I twigged and in some outrage enquired, 'What the fuck makes you think I am not a guest here?'

There was a collective silence and a lot of looking away, then one man stood up and said sternly, 'No need for that. Move on mate.'

Steve R. E. Pereira is a Melbourne-based Creative Producer working on performance and art-related community engagement and community development projects.

Chasing Unicorns | APRIL WHITE

Letter

RENEÉ BENNETT

To my family, friends and acquaintances …

This letter is difficult to write.

I am not well versed in overt discussion about deeply personal things; however I acknowledge that sometimes such communication is needed in order to foster understanding around particular experiences and to move forward in a positive way.

So I will do my best to articulate this.

For as long as I can remember, I have experienced a dissonance between my gender assigned at birth and my actual gender identity. I have spent almost as long trying to understand why.

In my mid-twenties, after a long road of self-reflection, I came to understand that I am a non-binary person, neither male nor female. I am just Reneé. With this epiphany came an immense sense of internal peace; which I can best equate to the relief one feels after carrying an awkwardly heavy object for a very long time, and then finally setting it down.

Since coming to this understanding, I have informally shared my gender identity with some of those around me; in fewer still I have confided how important it is to me to be treated as my authentic self. However, as time passes and non-strangers continue to refer to me using female pronouns, I have come to realise that an open and honest disclosure to everyone is an essential next step. For without sharing this part of myself, people are left only with their assumptions – they look at the external and default to labels ingrained in archaic societal conditioning. To assume is, like it or not, an inherent part of the human condition; therefore I cannot expect anyone to not default if I have never told them differently.

And so I have written this letter, as a form of 'formal' disclosure if you will, and to also respectfully make a request of my family, friends and acquaintances:

As a non-binary person, my preferred pronouns are 'they/them', and my official title is the gender-neutral 'Mx' – this has been changed (where currently possible) on almost all of my legal documents. Moving forward, I would wholeheartedly appreciate if people could please use my correct pronouns (and title where relevant). Calling me 'she/her' is not appreciated in any context. (I do have some close friends who call me 'brother' – I am okay with those particular friends continuing to do that).

I understand that this will be an adjustment for some people, and I am not expecting everyone to automatically and seamlessly adapt to this from the outset. The last thing I want is for people to be walking on egg shells around this. If you accidentally call me 'she', I am not going to get angry. All I ask is that you just try to be conscious of what I have expressed in this letter – such consciousness and consideration would mean the world to me.

I should also add, in the interest of full disclosure, that next year (2018) I will be undergoing chest reconstructive surgery to address an aspect of the dysphoria, which will allow my external to better represent my internal identity – I cannot express how positive I am about this endeavour. It is something that I have wanted since I was a child, and I am in no doubt that it will significantly improve my subjective experience of this reality. I have chosen to specifically include this update here, as I feel that this letter may help to provide some context for this impending external change (so it won't come as such a surprise when it happens).

Anyway, thank you for taking the time to read this – I appreciate you ☺

Nay

Mx Reneé Bennett is a non-binary person who – as many people have been recently choosing to do in the age of social media – came out through an online post during October 2017.

Safe Schools, Marriage Equality and LGBT Youth Suicide

SIMON COPLAND,
MARY LOU RASMUSSEN

Benjamin Law starts his Quarterly Essay, *Moral Panic 101*, with a powerful recollection of the suicide of Tyrone Unsworth, a thirteen year old Aboriginal boy from Queensland. We remember Unsworth's suicide as well. It was a tragedy that sent shockwaves through the Australian queer and Indigenous communities – a tragedy that to many seemed almost inevitable given the nature of the debate both on Safe Schools and marriage equality, and also because of high rates of youth suicide among LGBTI and Indigenous young people.

Yet, as we reflect on both of these debates it is important to critically engage with the relationship between queer people and mental health issues, particularly suicide. While it is important to acknowledge the impact systematic homophobia continues to have on mental health issues within queer and Indigenous communities, a narrative that inherently links these communities with mental health issues can be quite dangerous. This narrative has the potential to actively weaken our mental health, as well as the resilience of our communities and political movements.

The threat of mental health problems, and suicide in particular, has formed a large part of queer discourse in recent years. The defense of Safe Schools framed the program as an anti-bullying initiative, with the slogan 'Safe Schools Saves Lives' becoming common. Through this lens Safe Schools was seen as a program focused solely on getting kids through the tough times of queer childhood. It was about helping them to survive. Similar narratives have run throughout the debate on the postal survey on marriage equality. Opponents of the survey focused on the impact the ensuing debate would have on the mental health of queer Australians, in particular vulnerable youth. It has been treated as inevitable that any form of debate would hurt queer people, with Greens Senator Janet Rice at one point arguing that, 'it is no exaggeration to say that a plebiscite will mean that some people will feel that the best way forward is to take their own life.'

Mary Lou Rasmussen and Rob Cover (2017) have argued that linking non-heterosexuality and suicide has become a dominant narrative in popular culture, within and outside queer communities. We can see this throughout Australian culture at the moment. For example, Hannah Gadsby's award winning show *Nanette* has received accolades for her ability, in her own words, to 'take a story of woe from my actual factual life and make it hilarious.' Gadsby's show seems to have touched on a part of the queer psyche, with queers across the country relating to its content. In another example the comedian Magda Szubanski has increasingly spoken about the difficulties of her childhood, and was almost in tears on national television, saying she 'barely made it through my childhood.' Personal stories such as this are common within our debates, providing evidence for need for programs such as Safe Schools. Eve Sedgwick links this to perceptions of internalised shame, arguing that shame forms a foundational part of the queer experience, one which becomes 'contagious'. She argues that 'at least for certain ('queer') people, shame is simply the first, and remains a permanent, structuring fact of identity.'

It is this trend that we saw in Law's essay. By starting with Unsworth's suicide, Law's essay clearly rested on an association between queer youth and suicide. In doing so he treated the purpose of Safe Schools as being a program designed in large part to deal with this problem.

We are not arguing that homophobia does not exist in our modern society, that mental health problems and suicide are not an issue within the queer community, or that we should ignore issues of suicide. However, at the same time, we argue that we must be more careful and nuanced about how we deal with this issue, as we believe that the above framing is potentially making things worse.

Current debates which link queerness with mental health and suicide, we argue, treat queer people and communities as vulnerable and weak. It associates queer people with suicide in pathological way, taking away a significant amount of agency from queer people to both be happy, and to shape a positive future for ourselves. As queers we want to push against this narrative, because we think that it has the potential to heighten vulnerability in young people who are non-heterosexual identified.

We think that we must be careful about the linkage between queer kids and suicide, for while the numbers on this issue seem compelling, they remain heavily contested. Tom Waidzunas has written a persuasive paper about how the social problem of 'gay teen suicide' came to fruition in the US in the 1990s. He argues that the linking of queer people and suicide was based more on social needs than on hard data. This was backed up by a recent study by Richard Burns at the ANU, which suggested that lesbian, gay and bisexual people are not at major risk of poor mental health and suicide (Burns, Butterworth & Jorm, 2016). A systematic review of mental disorder and suicide in LGB people conducted in 2008 by Michael King *et al.* reports a higher risk but also points to the lower than expected prevalence of LGB populations in many of the surveys used in the review.

Even if suicide rates are higher within queer communities, we still argue that by treating ourselves as weak, vulnerable, and perennially suicidal we diminish the potential for the power and joy of the queer experience. It does so in two ways.

First this narrative treats queer people as weak and without agency. The framing of queer people as 'vulnerable' treats us as a community in need of help, help that largely comes from Governments, and other institutions. In political campaigning this has resulted in a focus of energy around campaigns for recognition (marriage equality) or protection (Safe Schools), two forms of state-based recognition that are increasingly framed as essential for our survival.

This, to us, runs counter to the potential of the queer community. Some of the most powerful moments of activism in queer communities in Australia, for example the first Mardi Gras, have occurred when queers have taken matters into their own hands. Queers have been required to build resilience through our own marginalisation, and it is through this resilience that queer communities have often managed our greatest achievements.

Secondly this framing of vulnerability treats queerness as an entirely depressing state. We could see this throughout the Safe Schools debate, in which queer childhood was often rendered in exclusively depressing terms. It was something that you survived, not something that allowed you to thrive.

This, at the most obvious level, denies the potential joy that can come from queerness, and denies it for queer youth in particular. There is much that is great about the queer community. Law highlighted this with his interviews with the young attendees of the same-sex formal. Throughout our history queers have actively created these positive contexts, turning queerness into a space of joy and creativity.

Treating queerness as inherently depressing also becomes reinforcing. The more we talk about how depressing being a queer young person can be, the more this can become embedded in the queer psyche. If we tell queer kids that life will always be hard, and that they should expect to be suicidal, the more likely it is that this will happen. We believe this has been particularly relevant during the debate on the marriage equality postal survey, in which a narrative of inherent-suffering has reinforced and amplified the negative experiences that have circulated around the debate.

We should be talking about the positives of the queer experience, ones framed around the queer community. It is this community that is often ignored, but is one that can provide both happiness, and a support network for those queer people who are experience homophobia.

We should be talking about the positives of the queer experience, ones framed around the queer community.

What is ironic is that the alternative to this approach was found within the Safe Schools program itself. As Law notes in his essay, the founders of Safe Schools aimed to get away from this negative narrative through positive messaging. Contrasting with the Beyond Blue's 2012 anti-homophobia campaign, which Law says 'featured gloomy, moodily lit portraits asking the public to *Imagine being made to feel crap for being left handed*, Safe Schools aimed to present a positive image of queer youth. As one of the co-founders of Safe Schools, Roz Ward, argued, 'It's not about bullying. The most effective way to reduce bullying around gender and sexuality is to have more positive and inclusive schools.'

If you look at the Safe Schools materials you can see this ethos play out. As Law notes the All of Us document features bright, happy, diverse and well-lit portraits of queer youth talking about their gender and sexuality in an affirming and inclusive manner. The program is designed to boost the potential of queer childhood, rather than to dampen it. This positive approach, although not without its flaws, we believe provided more value than one framed through the lens of vulnerability and mental health.

Given this, it was disappointing for us to see the campaign to protect Safe Schools focus so heavily on suicide and bullying. In fact this was the biggest failure of the campaign. First, it opened the program up to attacks, particularly when any conservative found parts of the program that were about inclusivity and positivity and not about bullying. If this program was just about bullying, then why was there so much positive and inclusive messaging within its materials? More importantly the campaign put queer Australians on the back foot. It immediately put queer youth in particular into a position of vulnerability, treating them as kids who needed to be protected. By talking about Safe Schools primarily through the lens of bullying, mental health, and in particular suicide, Law added to a discourse that is dominant within much of modern queer and mainstream discourse. In doing so he, inadvertently, once again took away agency from queer kids, treating them as those who need to be protected in order for them to survive.

_____

… queer youth are often resilient, creative, and determined to take matters into their own hands.

_____

Yet, while we've treated queer youth as inherently vulnerable, particularly during times of attack such as the campaign against Safe Schools, what we actually find is that queer youth are often resilient, creative, and determined to take matters into their own hands. Post the attacks on Safe Schools, programs akin to Safe Schools have emerged in public and private schools. As Law reports, in 2017, Edmund Rice Education Australia – an association of Catholic schools, has adapted the Safe Schools program for use in their schools. Luke Gahan, Tiffany Jones and Lynne Hiller (2014) reported that young gay people who are religious are demanding that their schools address issues related to gender and sexuality, and anticipate futures in which they will marry and have children.

Young people have also developed a myriad of resources related to sexuality and gender, which are readily accessible through platforms like Facebook, Instagram and Tumblr. Young people are demanding, producing and consuming resources related to gender and sexuality that reflect their interests and needs.

School-based education about gender and sexuality continues to have important symbolic relevance, especially for the parents of young people, but all young people (and especially those who are queer) understand that school is not the place where they are likely to obtain in-depth information about gender and sexuality. Additionally, the proliferation of queer resources outside formal education powerfully shapes young people's growing acceptance of, and demands for, recognition in curriculum and broader school cultures. These demands by young people preceded the Safe Schools debate and they will almost certainly continue to proliferate post this controversy, as well as post the debate related to the survey about marriage equality.

We do need to continue to recognise the impact homophobia has on Australian queer youth. Safe Schools was an important program designed to deal with these issues. At the same time, as queers, we need to work to disconnect the queer experience from suicide and vulnerability. As a community we are much stronger than this.

———————————

… we need to work to disconnect the queer experience from suicide and vulnerability. As a community we are much stronger than this.

———————————

Young people themselves are getting on with the job of creating platforms and places which help them to thrive and survive, far away from the brouhaha of marriage equality and Safe Schools. Law hints at this in his essay, but, unfortunately, reporting on these thriving queer youth cultures is much less newsworthy than reports pertaining to the abjection of queer youth. Frustratingly, these types of stories *and research* are more likely to attract media attention and government funding.

References

Burns, R., Butterworth, P., & Jorm, A. (2016). 'The long-term mental health risk associated with non-heterosexual orientation'. *Epidemiology and Psychiatric Sciences*. pp.1-10. Accessed 1.10.17. Retrieved from https://www.cambridge.org/core/journals/epidemiology-and-psychiatric-sciences/

Cover, R., Rasmussen, M., Aggleton, P. *et al.* (2017), 'Progress in question: the temporalities of politics support and belonging in gender-and sexually-diverse pedagogies', *Continuum: Journal of Media and Cultural Studies*, vol. Online, pp. 1-13.

Gahan, L., Jones, T. and Hillier, L. (2014). 'An Unresolved Journey: Religious Discourse and Same-sex Attracted and Gender Questioning Young People'. *The Social Scientific Study of Religion*. 25(1). pp.202-229.

Law, B. (2017). 'Moral Panic 101: Equality, Acceptance and the Safe Schools Scandal'. *Quarterly Essay*. 67. Accessed 1.10.17. Retrieved from: https://www.quarterlyessay.com.au/essay/2017/09/moral-panic-101

Simon Copland is a PhD candidate in Sociology at ANU. He is a freelance writer who has been published in the Guardian, SBS Online Australia, BBC Online, and co-produces and presents the podcast Queers. He is the co-editor of the online publishing site Green Agenda, and recently published a chapter in the book *How to Vote Progressive in Australia: Labor or Green?*

Professor Mary Lou Rasmussen is located in the School of Sociology at ANU. She is part of the ARC Discovery Project Queer Generations, investigating the experiences of two generations of LGBT young people in Australia. She is co-editor, with Louisa Allen, of the *Handbook of Sexuality Education* (2017, Palgrave) and her monograph, *Progressive Sexuality Education: The Conceits of Secularism* (2015, Routledge) has just been released in paperback.

So Two-Faced | GUY JAMES WHITWORTH

Pulling Memory

QUINN EADES

I remember: being so broke that when I went to the Hare Krishnas to get fed I didn't have five cents to drop into their coin box, and I'd take a beer bottle top with me just so I'd have something to put through the slot.

I remember: the sound the bottle top made when it hit the bottom: fraudulent, too light, a high click of thin metal meeting coin.

I remember: sitting on the floor with my food (always the same: curry, rice, semolina with spices and sultanas) and giving thanks. Hope the Hares weren't going to come and talk to me today, which was the real price of the food.

I remember: Zach sitting in the dirt eating yoghurt. Walking away to hang out the washing. Squinting at the midday sun. Looking behind me to see that Zach had finished his yoghurt and started on the dirt. His mouth, covered in a white smear of yoghurt pebbled with soil. His smile.

I remember: playing basketball in my new school shoes. Slippery soles. Shining too brightly. Missing a pass and getting hit in the nose, hard. Bursting into tears and running into the girls' bathroom and hiding inside a toilet cubicle. Being small enough to sit on the ground between toilet and door. Holding my knees. Sobbing. Looking at black shoe leather shining in the dusky light.

I remember: driving to the writing workshop this morning feeling anxious about what I had to offer.

I remember: watching *Star Trek* last night (stoned and warm and alone) and grinning at the screen. So good, my head kept saying, so good.

I remember: telling her I was leaving. Telling her I was trans. Telling her I was bent. Telling her I was queer. Telling her I needed to write. Telling her I wasn't mad.

Quinn Eades is a researcher, writer, and award-winning poet whose work lies at the nexus of feminist, queer and trans theories of the body, autobiography, and philosophy. He is published nationally and internationally, and is the author of *all the beginnings: a queer autobiography of the body*, and *Rallying*. Eades is also the winner of the 2017 Arts Queensland XYZ Award for Innovation in Spoken Word, and he is currently working on a book-length collection of fragments written from the transitioning body, titled *Transpositions*.

This Writing Life

ERROL BRAY

Writing-wise, this year started pretty well. My second novel *The Quarters* had been out for a month. All through January the New Farm Library (in Brisbane, the hellishly hot city where I am compelled to live) had an exhibition of my Collage Diaries. I have kept these diaries for 40 years. They don't contain much writing, just pictures, news items, drawings, photos, that I find in various magazines and paste into the A4 desk-diary. They also have artwork from the various projects I've done over the years and stuff from my travels and from shows and movies I've seen.

The first diary, 1978, has a picture of New York in blackout on the cover and Mick Jagger on the inside cover; p.3 has twenty-two pictures almost all black & white (Orson Welles, Monroe & Clift, two Tom of Finland drawings, Paul Robeson, Rudolf Valentino, and more). The diaries are short on words and the pictures often cluster into subjects or themes across a 2-page spread each time. In my current diary I have a page dedicated to Sam Shepard. I made small photocopies of the covers of all the books I own about him and glued these in.

Over the last few months there have been lots of cuttings about the Equal Marriage campaign and over the past several years lots of material about climate change.

Every Thursday I went into the new Farm Library and turned each diary to a new page so people got some variety. The librarian loved them and asked me to give a talk which would include a reading from

The Quarters and a chance to sell copies. It was a nice night but one of the attendees pointed out that people frequent libraries to borrow books, not buy them. He was right!

However, members of the Queer Readers Club which meets at the library did buy several copies when I gave a little talk to them. It helped that I had been a member of the Club for five years I guess. The amazingly well-read member of QRC who does a Blog each month reviewing 7 or 8 books each time gave *The Quarters* a well-considered review and pronounced it a good read and entertaining.

Then there was the big launch night for *The Quarters* (organised by LGBTIQ friend and helper Tracey Cranitch) in March at Avid Reader in West End. They charge a modest fee but, wow, do they deliver. It was a terrific night. Lots of friends and strangers attending, tasty nibblies and very drinkable wine, and some sales! I was lucky to have internationally acclaimed writer Angela Slatter as Chair and she did a great job with a Q&A session, even made me appear to be semi-coherent. I've known Angela since before she was a 'somebody' and I was less than a nobody and we both worked at QUT. (Buy her books of stories and her new novel *Vigil*. They are great!) An idea of our respective statuses in writing occurred when I asked her if her novel (which I bought in paperback) was also in a hard cover edition. She said, a touch haughtily perhaps, 'Errol, all my books are in hard covers.' I must have a word with my publisher.

Okay, what about the rest of the year? No mention of actual writing yet. When I finish a novel I usually have a period of two-three weeks with no ideas in my brain and a panicky feeling that I'll never write another one. Then one morning I wake up and there it is - popped up into consciousness with many of the most important elements in place. I make notes. I embark on sketchy research, if necessary. Take care. Sometimes interesting research can replace actual writing. So once *The Quarters* went into its intensive editing stage in early 2016, there was not much panic because I already had the idea of the *next* novel in my head, along with the question of how humans will deal with the worst case possible scenario of climate change, plus throwing in an asteroid storm and a small atomic war. At present it's called *Oracle Odyssey: 2121*. I've spasmodically been writing it during last year and this year. Look for it in about three or four years – unless the events I describe overtake us.

In December I will be visiting Frankfurt and Edinburgh for research as they are the two most important outposts of civilisation dealt with in the novel. What a good excuse for my almost annual travel indulgence, which will involve Paris and London too. When you think of yourself as a writer all sorts of indulgences seem reasonable.

Speaking of indulgences, I spent a lot of fun time this year writing a musical comedy. I know it's unusual for a gay man to like musical comedy. But. It was pretty much a waste of time. I enjoyed it immensely and it gave me an excuse to go to Sydney to pitch the idea at an event at the Hayes Theatre. The professional theatre folk providing feedback there pointed out some home truths, which I already knew but had ignored, about the hugely unlikely chances of even finding a composer to do music for the songs, let alone finding any company prepared to develop the sort of project that Broadway does so brilliantly. A guilty indulgence now ensconced in the 'archives' folder.

Along with Tracey and her partner, Siana (an IT wiz), I've been exploring the idea of becoming an e-book publisher. There are novels I like from 25 years ago which have been rejected by everybody and a couple of novellas which I'm fond of. Novellas don't tend to get published except when famous names write them.

I often feel as if we need a lawyer sitting in when we're filling out some of the e-publishing forms. Also, marketing your own electronic works is a real mystery to us at present, but there's lots of advice available online. If this sounds as if a writing life involves a great deal of organisational fiddling, that's because it does. Every platform, every competition has different requirements. My least favourite question is when they ask you to compare your novel with something else that's been published. My temptation is to say, 'But, *my* novel is unique.'

Given the above, the obvious question is: why don't you give up? Are you mad? No! Why would I give up an occupation that allows me to buy lots of books? My library has 4,000 items in it and still breeding. Why would I give up something that forces me to travel for research and inspiration? Why would I give up a way of life that lets me do anything I want while using the excuse of developing my creativity? Why would I give up something I love so much? And last week I woke up with a platypus in my brain and am now planning out a lovely adventure book for kids.

Errol Bray has worked in theatre for forty years as playwright, director, arts administrator, festival director, youth arts worker, lecturer/tutor. He was founding Artistic Director of Shopfront Theatre for Young People, Sydney (1976-1985); of World Interplay festival for young playwrights (1983-1995); of the Emerge Project, Brisbane (2005-1012) for development of new playwrights. His plays have been produced internationally, most recently *The Choir* (2009) in London. His debut novel, *Berzoo*, was published in 2011 and *The Quarters* in 2016.

Freedom

BLAIR ARCHBOLD

When puberty began for me I decided I'd rather die than live past my eighteenth birthday. I could get through high school as a tomboy (barely), but I was not doing womanhood. It felt like the decision had been made for me by something bigger than myself. It terrified me but it also gave me a weird sense of relief. *I will kill myself before I turn eighteen.*

I told no one. I had no one to tell.

Before I transitioned from female to male I used to feel like a big portion of the real me lived in an attic. This attic was somewhere above my body, a hidden room no one else could see. I would have visions of myself writing in this space, books stacked in piles all over the place, thinking always, *It's not safe to go back.* My body was an avatar suit meant for another and as much as I tried to leave, there was a part of me trapped inside, forced to interact with the world as female.

Late at night when I was trying to sleep a tsunami would suddenly surge up within me. It was like Katsushika Hokusai's *The Great Wave of Kanagawa*, and there I was in the water, no boat, no life jacket, silently panicking. Again and again the wave would find me in my nightmares. Always I was trying to run. Always I couldn't move fast enough. The truth is I felt the wave even in my mother's womb. It wasn't coming from within me. It wasn't even coming from my mother. It was an ancestor. He wanted me dead.

For months leading up to my chest surgery I felt something coming. People said, 'Don't worry, it's a standard procedure, everything will be fine'. I didn't know how to explain it but I felt like I was going to die. Then I nearly did. No one could explain why a standard complication like a hematoma had led to me nearly bleeding out on the table. The surgeon said he'd never seen anything like it.

One night during the early years of my transition I was walking late at night down the street and a woman crossed the road to avoid me. It was the first time I'd experienced being perceived as a threat because I had been read as male. I felt awful that she saw me that way but I had also been in her shoes and I knew there was a reason why a woman crossed a street at night to avoid a man. In that moment I felt the weight of something ancient in the space between us, old as god.

Someone asked me not that long ago, 'Do you notice other men are threatened by your ability to be vulnerable?' The kind of masculinity that's valuable to me is one that's about integrity, honesty and having the courage to live your life in a way that embodies who you really are. It takes courage to be seen. It takes strength to be vulnerable. When I first started transitioning I wanted a male role model. Someone who embodied the kind of masculinity I'd feel comfortable with, and I couldn't find one anywhere.

I was once told that darkness is the place we go to reset. It is the womb of the Mother. Sometimes it can feel like death but we need to die to something if we want to change. I have died many times, which is just another way of saying I have changed many times. I have shed my skin the way the snake does to become more myself.

Growing up, I watched the women in my family suffer in silence and because I was embodied in a female form I was expected to do the same. One thing I've learned, women are more powerful than they know. They bleed and do not die.

Blair Archbold has contributed writing and voiceover work as an inspiring trans community leader, including as a co-host on *3CR's Out of the Pan: Sally Goldner and Blair Archbold.*

Queer/ing Objects?

NIKKI SULLIVAN
CRAIG MIDDLETON

Recent research has shown that the stories and experiences of lesbian, gay, bisexual, transgender, intersex, and queer (LGBTIQ+) people are largely absent in museums internationally, and that this negatively impacts LGBTIQ+ people, their families and allies in a wide range of ways. At the same time, there is a growing awareness in the GLAM (Galleries, Libraries, Archives, and Museums) sector that publically funded cultural institutions have a duty to reflect diversity in all its forms, to take an active approach to inclusion, and to promote understanding between different groups, communities and cultures.

Objects, as Oliver Winchester notes, 'are the lifeblood of a museum' (2012, p.145). As social history museum curators, we collect, document, preserve, display, and interpret 'historical' objects in order to tell stories about the pasts that contribute to the present in which we now find ourselves. But like the vast majority of other museum collections, ours includes very few objects that are catalogued using terms such as lesbian, gay, transgender, homosexual, queer, and so on. We have consequently struggled with the question of how to tell LGBTIQ+ inclusive his/stories without such objects (or at least, without objects that are identified as such, and are therefore 'at hand'). One of the aims of our organisation's LGBTIQ+ Inclusion Action Plan is to actively collect LGBTIQ+ objects. Our LGBTIQ+ Inclusion Action Plan draws on the vision and values of our parent organisation - The History Trust of South Australia - and implements its strategic plan as it pertains to LBGTIQ+ visitors, staff, programs, engagement, and collections. However, as we've discovered, this raises questions of what a 'queer' object is. We have chosen to use the term 'queer' for two reasons. First, it can, and often is, used as an umbrella term for LGBTI+, and second, it can also be used as a verb, to queer. In our practice we aim both to collect objects through which the stories of marginalised groups might be explored, and, at the same time, to challenge the taxonomies, processes, and powers of privilege employed by large collecting institutions.

Questions about what a 'queer object' might be include:

- Should an object be considered queer because the person who made it identifies as such or is presumed to have been gay or lesbian: for example, Michelangelo's 'David'?
- Should an object be considered queer because the donor or lender of the object is queer-identified?
- Should an object be considered queer because a well-known transgender person purchased, commissioned, or used it?
- Should an object be considered queer if it depicts what we understand as same-sex intimacy: for example, the Warren Cup (British Museum) which could be read as depicting males in mutual sex acts?
- Should an object be considered queer because it was used in the management of queer issues or lives for better or worse: for example, the postal survey mailed to our letter-boxes, or the pink triangle used in Auschwitz?

Rather than regarding these as questions with definitive answers, we view them as an opportunity to explore the nature of meaning: is meaning inherent in an object, or is it an effect of meaning-making practices that are situated in a particular historical and cultural context? Drawing on the work of poststructuralist and queer theorists, we are convinced that the latter is the case. After all, if you think about it, 'objects displayed with only minimal interpretation can rarely speak for themselves' (Winchester, 2012, p.145): this is particularly true of unusual objects. On the other hand, extremely familiar objects often bring with them connotations or associations that might be at odds with the interpretation that the curator intends the viewer to take away. This is why, in social history museums, objects tend to be accompanied by detailed labels that 'tell a story' of what the curator and/or the museum believe to be the object's significance, and sometimes, its provenance. This is contrary to art museums that often take a different approach to object labels. Art museums will often include details of maker, manufacturer, medium, and so on, but don't necessarily 'tell a story' or explain meaning in ways that social history museums attempt to do. Traditionally, the aim of labels has been to present what were assumed to be objective facts to the viewer, however, the meaning-making function of labels is increasingly being recognised by museum professionals, as is the political nature of display. There is also an awareness of the fact that the framing of objects - the context in which they are displayed, their placement in relation to other objects, etc. - contributes to the interpretations made by viewers.

Meaning-making has also come to be understood as an ongoing, generative process that involves viewers as much as it does those who create displays. Despite curators' best efforts to classify and interpret objects - perhaps even to determine their meaning - visitors bring to museum visits past experiences, dispositions, idea(l)s, and opinions that colour their interpretation of objects on display, their significance, and the stories they might tell. Recognition of this heterogeneous process 'queers' the colonialist view of the museum as a place of education that provides access to truths that visitors may otherwise never encounter. It also replaces the figure of the passive viewer who simply consumes what is presented to them, with a notion of 'publics' - diverse individuals and groups who are engaged, intelligent, co-creators in the processes of world-making both within and outside the museum. At the same time, engaged and engaging museums have come to see themselves as sites of discussion and debate, as forums for ideas rather than repositories for 'static' objects. In this changing vision objects become vehicles for exploring ideas, discussing issues, situating debate, rather than things of significance in themselves.

If meaning is made through an interactive relationship between curators, objects, viewers, and contexts (both within and beyond the museum), rather than residing in an object, then it is impossible to define - at least in any absolute sense - what is, and what is not, a queer object. At the same time though, it is possible to track connections between particular objects and specific individuals, events, and so on. For example, we can know that a 'yes' badge in our collection was one of many that were produced and distributed by The Equality Campaign, a joint initiative of Australian Marriage Equality and Australians for Equality, during the postal vote that recently took place. And we may well use this badge in future exhibitions that track the changing legal status of same-sex acts, relationships, rights, and so on, or that tell stories of grassroots political movements. In short, it is possible, and sometimes useful, to name an object *as* 'queer', just as it is possible, and sometimes useful, to use an object *to* 'queer', that is, to trouble what we might understand as normative curatorial practices. These different, but not necessarily incompatible, approaches are being used with increasing frequency in museums internationally.

For example, in recent years large international museums including the British Museum and the Victoria and Albert Museum have identified objects such as letters, sculptures, prints, pottery, silverware, and so on, as 'evidence' of same-sex desire and gender diversity in other times and places. This revealing of 'hidden', 'repressed' or 'marginalised' histories undoubtedly has an important role to play in challenging heteronormative historical narratives and assumptions about the ahistorical, universal, and thus 'natural' status of heterosexuality, however, but tends not to challenge, in any fundamental way, the taxonomies, curatorial practices and processes, and powers of privilege that underpin large collecting institutions.

Rather than simply representing objects as queer, UK-based artist and curator Matt Smith has used objects and object labels to queer practices of display. Smith questions and critiques decisions made by curators by 're-appropriating objects to tell revised stories, removing objects from the stores and placing them centre stage and placing newly created 'historic' objects within the collection to fill LGBT gaps' (2005, p.103). The three main techniques Smith employs in projects such as *Queering the Museum* (featured at the Birmingham Museum and Art Gallery, 2011) are relabeling; juxtaposition (placing an object next to another to cast it in a new/alternative light); and the creation of new art/works that reconfigure the meaning of the existing objects with which they are displayed. For example, Smith displayed a taxidermied otter from Birmingham Museum and Art Gallery's natural history collection in close proximity with three small ceramic bears which he created. The juxtaposition of these creatures troubles conventional taxonomies (the idea that, for example, scientific collections are different to natural history collections, and to decorative arts collections, all of which are conventionally displayed and stored separately), and, at the same time, resignifies the otter. This is achieved in part by the accompanying labels which read:

Stereotypes: Bears are larger, hairy gay men who often have beards. Otters are slimmer hairy gay men. They are sometimes seen playing together in the wild.

In conclusion, then, we suggest that while it is important for curators to take an active role in the classification and reclassification of objects relating to LGBTIQ+ lives. Where possible, we might also work to queer museological practice and the material effects it produces.

References

Smith Matt, 2015, Making Things Perfectly Queer, Doctor of Philosophy, University of Brighton, UK (unpublished PhD thesis). Accessed: 16/11/17. Retrieved from: http://eprints.brighton.ac.uk/15556/1/Complete%20E%20Dissertation%20Jan%202016.pdf

Winchester, O. (2012) 'A book with its pages always open?', in *Museums, Equality and Social Justice*, R. Sandell & E. Nightingale (eds.), London: Routledge, pp.142-55.

Nikki Sullivan (Migration Museum) and Craig Middleton (Centre of Democracy) are curators working in social history museums part of the History Trust of South Australia - a statutory authority responsible for South Australia's state history collections and interpretation. Nikki is also Honorary Associate Professor of Critical and Cultural Studies in the Department of Media, Music, Communication and Cultural Studies at Macquarie University.

In Memoriam:
Graham Carbery
1947-2017

DANIEL MARSHALL

Graham Carbery, partner of Gary Jaynes for 45 years and founder of the
Australian Lesbian and Gay Archives, died on 5 July 2017 at Box Hill
Hospital. As founder of the Archives in 1978, Graham was a visionary
and a pioneer. In the 1970s, many Australians found it difficult to accept
that homosexuals existed in society; the idea that there might be
something like a gay and lesbian history of Australia was, for many
people (including many homosexuals at the time), an even more remote
possibility. This was an idea that many people simply did not even
contemplate. The Archives helped to change that. Four decades since its
founding ALGA stands as the most comprehensive historical collection
of Australian LGBTIQ material anywhere in the world.

Built from within the social and activist communities whose histories
the Archives preserves, Graham and other likeminded people invented
new ways for collecting and preserving historical materials. When they
started this work they did not have a manual for how to do it, they had
to make it up as they went along. By building a community of volunteers
in Australia and forging international links with others engaged in similar
work, they built an institution which has endured.

The Archives they created became a space that nurtured a consciousness or curiosity about history, sexuality, gender and difference. Like so many other people, I first got to know Graham through him helping me to navigate the Archives' collection in some early research that I was doing. That introduction to the Archives changed my life, as the lives of so many others have been changed: it helped inspire us to join the work of preserving and remembering the past. The impact of Graham's achievements cannot easily be measured because they ripple out into so many people's lives.

Unpaid and unheralded, Graham's labour of a lifetime is a profound gift to all of us. By working to save our history he has helped give the gift of the past to the future so that tomorrow's young people will be able to know the struggles and the celebrations that have brought us to where we are. This is a debt that can never be repaid.

Graham lived a rich and vibrant life. As an umpire he stood up against homophobia decades before the AFL's pride game, and as a writer and researcher in gay and lesbian history, he helped to grow the field of gender and sexuality studies in Australia. In August, Graham's friends from both the LGBTIQ and umpiring communities, as well as his neighbours and past colleagues, gathered together in the Fitzroy Community Room overlooking the WT Peterson Oval to share their grief and loss, and to extend their love to Gary and to Graham's relatives. It was a beautiful day, and the love of that day shines brightly. Fittingly, from time to time, a bit of the noise from the footy game going on outside would filter inside – an umpire's whistle, a rowdy crowd barracking hard. As we said on the day – he would have loved that.

Next year the Archives turns forty, and we will keep on missing him. We will miss his generosity, humour, knowledge and passion. He cannot be replaced, but we can honour his legacy by continuing the work, and through the work his memory will endure.

———————

Daniel Marshall is a past president of the Australian Gay and Lesbian Archives. *Bent Street* welcomes suggested contributions about admired members of our community who have passed in our year of publication.

Inspired Insomnia | APRIL WHITE

Lys Mediterranae

NADIA BAILEY

Hanna moves into my house in late spring. She has the room on the top floor, with its wooden floors and shifting sunlight. She brings an antique bed and a sad-eyed black dog. She wears lipstick the colour of cut blood oranges and her tattoos suggest an impulsive streak. She asks me questions with such guileless ease that I find myself revealing details of my life, that under normal circumstances, I would hesitate to tell my closest friends. Every Sunday morning, we have coffee together. At the café, we talk, or we don't talk. We sit. We drink our coffee. Time slows, or maybe it quickens. This is the way love happens.

In text messages, she nicknames me 'Chicken'. English is her third language, after Polish and Greek. On the phone to her brother Jakub, her rapid Polish has the lilt and cadence of birdsong. Her manners are elaborate. She is generous with her money to the same extent that I am uncomfortable with it: *Oh please*, she says, if I try to split the bill after dinner. *I wouldn't dream of it.* And if I persist: *Please, you'll embarrass me.*

Hanna is estranged from her family, all except for her younger brother. The two of them are close in a way that makes me feel diminished. In place of the family she was born into, she has a family of her own making: her ex-girlfriend, Harriet, with whom she remains close, her brother, Jakub, and her boyfriend, Daniel. Daniel has a long, serious face and long, coltish limbs. He's training to be a carpenter. He is soft spoken, and wry, and I am so jealous of him that sometimes I can't breathe.

When he cheats on her, somewhere in Europe with an older woman, Hanna retreats to her room and I don't see her for days. When she emerges, she's angry. She spits venom at him, halfway around the world. They exchange long emails. She gives me some of them to read, and the thrill of broken privacy makes me weak at the knees.

Daniel comes home. They talk. She tells me that they're trying to make it work. It's summer. The magnolias are dropping armfuls of white petals all over the street and the air smells like rotten sweetness.

Weeks pass. Hanna goes to stay at Daniel's house. I feel certain that they will break up. Instead, she calls me and says: *Daniel and I are engaged. We're celebrating tonight, will you come?* So we — her family — go out to dinner to celebrate. We offer congratulations. Hanna wears a dress the colour of the ocean at its most fathomless. She sits under Jakub's arm, and leans into his shoulder. Harriet says little. I bring lilies, which leave yellow pollen all over the tablecloth. Despite everything, Daniel looks happy.

After dinner, Hanna and I walk back to our house in the mellow, end-of-summer evening. Just the two of us, and all the things we're not saying. When we get home, we linger outside her bedroom. Eventually, she says: *It's about committing to the relationship. Committing to each other.* She says: *Just because we're engaged, it doesn't mean we'll get married.* And then she says: *I don't want to be alone tonight.*

Lying next to Hanna, in her bed, I commit her profile to memory. Black fringe swooping down to touch her eyelashes. The shape of her mouth in the even breath of sleep. A smudge of mascara bruising her inner elbow. I'm as close to her as I've ever been. She's still wearing the dress she wore to dinner, and one strap has slipped from her shoulder and dangles like an open parentheses.

I don't sleep. I don't move. I listen to her breathe.

By dawn, the air is hot and thick and dull. I feel feverish. I slip from bed and step softly from the room. Outside, it's cooler. Grey morning light. I splash my face with water, bent over the sink, and come up feeling sure.

When I open the door to Hanna's room, I see the blankets pushed back into a wild tangle at the foot of the bed. The sheets expose the ghost of where we lay.

Hanna is standing in front of the mirror, eyes rubbed clean of sleep, hair swept up into an efficient topknot. She's changed her clothes. She says: *How did you sleep?* and her voice is bright, and brisk, and final.

Nadia Bailey is a writer and freelance arts and culture journalist based in Sydney. She writes both long-form and short-form reviews, essays, and opinion pieces, typically focusing on literature, art, music and film. Nadia has worked on the editorial team of magazines such as *Oyster* and *Vogue Australia*. In 2017, she joined the Sydney Writers' Festival as Digital Marketing Coordinator. http://www.nadiabailey.com/

Back to the Ghetto

DOUG POLLARD

BLOG. FIRST PUBLISHED IN THESTIRRER.COM.AU 21 MARCH 2017

St Kilda has long had a reputation as a raffish, down-at-heel place, a 'haunt', as the saying goes, of marginalised people. It is for this reason it still hosts Melbourne's Pride March.

> Densely populated postwar St Kilda became Melbourne's red light district, home to low-cost rooming houses. Since the late 1960s, St Kilda has become known for its culture of bohemians and as home to many prominent artists, musicians and subcultures, including punk and LGBT. While some of these groups still maintain a presence in St Kilda, in recent years the district has experienced rapid gentrification pushing many lower socio-economic groups out to other areas. (Wikipedia)

The government would like to 'revive' St Kilda, and in particular Fitzroy Street, which is frankly the rough end of the burb. It houses the crumbling apartment building The George, which is plagued by drug users shooting up on the fire escapes, and sex workers taking advantage of its lax security to entertain their clients in its hallways.

It is also the site of the Gatwick Hotel, shortly to be closed to undergo 'The Block' treatment by Channel 9. The Gatwick has a long (and horrible) history as a dangerous home of last resort for people with nowhere else to go, a crime, drugs and sex work hotspot. Across the street from the Gatwick stands the proposed site of the Pride Centre.

> The Centre will be based at 79–81 Fitzroy Street in St Kilda and will be offered on a freehold basis provided it operates there for the next 20 years. The state government has invested $15 million into the Centre as part of its major $29 million budget package towards LGBTI projects and initiatives (https://www.premier.vic.gov.au/).

The decision has met with a mixed response. On the one hand it is abundantly clear that the city desperately needs a Pride Centre to provide a safe secure home for the myriad gay organisations based here. On the other hand, from other perspectives it looks very much like the state government wants to move the gay community out of the city centre and back into its old ghetto in St Kilda.

On the other hand, from other perspectives it looks very much like the state government wants to move the gay community out of the city centre and back into its old ghetto in St Kilda.

There is a perfect city centre location which once looked like becoming the Pride Centre by default. In 2007 the City of Melbourne offered space in an office block it no longer needed to community organisations, at half commercial rents. LGBTI radio station Joy 94.9 took the entire top floor, with another floor taken by the now-defunct ALSO Foundation. Sundry smaller organisations leased space from ALSO.

The building, an art deco mini-skyscraper in Bourke St that was once the ComBank HQ, was rechristened The City Village. It's in the

CBD, close to the retail heart, business district, and metro stations, with trams running past the door. Which is why the City would now like its building back. The lure of commercialising such a prime city centre location is just too much.

I am thrilled beyond measure that we have such a generous and supportive state government willing to back a Pride Centre with cash and political clout. I am pleased they appointed a Board that appears to be highly professional and competent. But I think that Board set the wrong selection criteria and in consequence have chosen the wrong location.

Access is problematic. Fitzroy Street has trams, it's true, but it's a 30-45 minute ride from Flinders St. There is no metro station within walking distance. And for the more affluent (even though they may be less likely to need or use the centre) who can drive there, parking is limited, and expensive.

Once upon a time, St Kilda, because of its rundown character, was something of an LGBTI enclave. Small apartments and bedsits were available cheap. Those days are long gone. Gentrification has seen many old buildings replaced with swish and expensive new blocks, and subdivided houses reunified. Spiralling rents across the city have forced most LGBTI well out of the city. Daniel Reeders has summed up the problem:

Locating the Pride Centre in St Kilda ignores the needs of queer people in emerging population centres in the West, the outer North, and the outer South-East. The Pride Centre **must** be located near a major train station, within easy reach of the centre of Melbourne's hub-and-spoke transit network. In creating a centre to celebrate the triumph of queer community over historical inequities, the Andrews Government should not be creating new ones.[1]

The Board should never even have shortlisted locations that were not close to a City Loop metro station. Siting the Pride Centre in St

---

[1] https://badblood.wordpress.com/2017/03/18/place-of-pride/

Kilda is not a step forward, but back. Back to the time when St Kilda was a cheap and affordable home for LGBTI people. A gay ghetto.

The government hopes that, along with the gentrification of the Gatwick, it will lift the reputation of the area, attract new businesses and revive existing ones. Probably gay ones. The tourism industry would love to turn Fitzroy Street into a Gay Destination, a 'Castro-On-Sea,' a new stop for the tour buses come to gawp at the queers.

This is on a par with the usual marginalisation of our community: Pride March is stuffed safely out of sight on Fitzroy St.; Midsumma, after an abortive break out into central locations, is once more back in the scruffy patch of land called Alexandra Gardens. And now Joy 94.9 looks likely to be exiled from the CBD too.

I repeat, I'm thrilled we're getting a centre, something I have long wished for. I just wish they would put it in the city where it belongs, instead of bribing us to go back to a shiny new ghetto.

———————————

Doug Pollard is an author on *The Stirrer* and broadcasts *The Rainbow Report* in Melbourne with Joy 94.9. You can follow The Rainbow Reporter on Facebook and Twitter @rainbowreporter.

Everyone's a Critic | GUY JAMES WHITWORTH

Cancer Screening

LUCILLE KERR
TIFFANY JONES

Cancer Screening for the Trans and Gender Diverse Community

Invisibility, Emerging Visibility, and the Need for Change

Cancer is the leading cause of death in Australia – half of men and a third of women will have had this disease by the time they are 85 [1]. Trans and gender diverse people are largely invisible in cancer literature, research, and registries [2]. Indeed, so much cancer literature presumes people have gender normative experiences; talks about body parts in highly gendered ways; and overlooks the issues related to gender-affirming treatments or other issues specifically relevant to trans and gender diverse people. Gender-affirming medical and/or surgical technologies can influence cancer risk and screening [3]. A few researchers have begun to argue that as more people present at younger ages for gender-affirming hormone treatment there may be an increase in cancer over time [3-5]. However, as there have been few studies that address the affects that medical and/or surgical transition have on cancer, the extent to which trans and gender diverse people are at risk of developing this disease remains unknown [6]. There is a lack of adequate evidence and general discussion on this issue, and as a result there are no policies, clinical guidelines, or resources in Australia dedicated to cancer care in the trans and gender diverse community. With the long-standing invisibility of gender diversity evolving into an emerging visibility, there is a need for change within cancer services.

Diverse Diversities

The use of umbrella terms around gender identity can result in the mistaken belief that trans and gender diverse people are an homogenous group, but this is far from the reality. Individuals express their gender in many ways, and one trans man may have significantly different life experiences when compared with another trans man, brotherboy, a trans woman, sistergirl, genderqueer person, or any other gender nonconforming person [7]. The word 'cancer' may also seem to suggest one phenomena; however hundreds of different malignant tumours can originate from vastly different cells in the human body – producing distinct and unique types [8]. In thinking about cancer care for Australia's trans and gender diverse community, we must therefore throw away over-generalisations that simply do not represent the diversity of human experience. We must instead see this topic as complex, requiring a broader research base which will help healthcare professionals to provide appropriate, sensitive, and timely services, and inform outreach to community members to improve their knowledge and access.

Why Is This Issue Urgent?

The Australian trans and gender diverse community's health and wellbeing are adversely affected by relatively high rates of homelessness, familial rejection, social isolation, alcohol or substance abuse, low socioeconomic status, anxiety, depression, self-harm, and suicide risk [5, 9-13]. Broadly, these experiences are a result of stigma and discrimination, cisgenderism (the delegitimisation of genders and bodies that do not fit cultural norms of gender/sex), and the lack of access to gender-affirming treatments [14]. Trans and gender diverse Australians have mixed experiences with our healthcare system, including experiencing inconsistency in services and an invisibility of gender diversity [13, 15]. Those who live rurally or remotely have less access to key services [16, 17], whilst many trans and gender diverse people report professionals showing persistent misconceptions and prejudices [12, 13, 18]. Many individuals therefore delay or avoid accessing services or disclosing their gender identity [12]. This is particularly concerning in terms of cancer, because early detection is the best defence against serious illness.

On top of all of this, cancer journeys themselves can be truly overwhelming, and if you already experience many disparities in your health care and social support, it may be even more complicated. People commonly respond to diagnoses with intense feelings of distress, isolation and vulnerability, with their mortality being called into question [19]. Diagnostic testing is an uncertain and anxious time, and rapidly progresses to the treatment phase [20]. Therapies commonly take a sledge-hammer approach, leading to side effects from nausea and vomiting to bone marrow suppression [21]. Long-term side effects may persist for years after treatment ends, and periodic check-ups to see whether or not disease has recurred can be stressful [19]. Approximately a third of cancer patients die within five years of diagnosis, and end of life care is a fundamental aspect of oncology care [1]. Patients are immersed in the medical world, forced to learn the jargon, navigate specialist services, and interact with many healthcare workers [19].

'Gendered' or 'sexed' cancers and screening procedures may pose particular problems for those who find certain body parts distressing or feel disassociated from them [22]. Trans and gender diverse people may use their own terms for such organs, and medical environments and professionals may not be aware of, or respect these. Added to this is the fact that mainstream services may make trans and gender diverse people and their loved ones feel alienated and unwelcome [6]. Distress around these issues can lead to under-attendance to cancer care services [23]. It is vital that these issues are addressed by the people working within this area so that the trans and gender diverse community can benefit from prevention and screening programs to the same degree that cisgender individuals do.

How Can We Overcome This?

The LGBTIQA+ community (inclusive of lesbian, gay, bisexual, transgender, intersex, queer, asexual, and allies) has a strong history of advocacy, and is capable of influencing impressive change. The concept of 'patient-centred care', which is a highly used term in medical services today, was directly influenced by the LGBTIQA+ community pushing for the rights and better treatment of people with HIV/AIDS since the 1980s [24]. Incredible progress has been made in both the social and medical treatment of people with HIV/AIDS, and the LGBTIQA+ community's passion, creativity, and activism played a major part in this. This community is capable of spirited mobilisation around an issue, with a unique understanding of the need for positivity, sensitivity, and vivacity. There is a critical need for research that examines the provision of oncology services to trans and gender diverse people – as currently these individuals are not receiving equitable cancer care [2, 25, 26]. Barriers and facilitators should be highlighted, along with the current experiences and needs of trans and gender diverse cancer patients. The findings of such studies need to be shared throughout oncology services, and within trans and gender diverse communities and networks, in order to improve health and enhance social justice. We should also identify and draw on a range of the strengths of Australian trans and gender diverse communities as they relate to healthcare. By building on these strengths, we may be able to supplement the gaps between all the pink and blue campaigns which so clearly provide wonderful supports and aid for cisgender and typically bodied females and males. In short, trans and gender diverse people deserve so much better care and consideration than they are getting.

Love Yourself, Screen Yourself

Beyond and whilst working on research and improvements to the Australian healthcare system, we need to encourage regular cancer screening for our trans and gender diverse friends, lovers, parents, siblings, extended family, mentors, and mentees - and (where relevant) one's self. A basic awareness of the signs and symptoms associated with cancer is a good starting point; however, it is important to keep in mind that many of these may be related to more common and less serious health issues. Gender affirming treatment may even cause some of these symptoms. Such signs and symptoms include the following; lumps, bumps, irregularities, sores, or ulcers out of the ordinary; a cough that does not go away or with blood present; ongoing hoarseness; unexplained weight loss; moles that have changed in their appearance; a change in toilet habits that continues for an extended period (loose bowels, constipation, bleeding, discoloured faeces); problems/changes in urination; unusual changes in your chest/breast tissue; any unexpected bleeding from a frontal opening/vagina; and for individuals with ovaries, persistent pain or bloating in the abdomen [27]. These symptoms may or may not indicate the presence of cancer, but it is important to discuss them with your doctor anyway. Organs which may be uncomfortable to think of as a part of your body can still develop cancer. It is important to pay attention to these organs, or ask a health professional, partner, or friend to look at them for you.

Cancer Screening for Chest/Breast Tissue

The current BreastScreen recommendation is that women between the ages of 50 and 74 have a mammogram (an x-ray of the breast) once every two years [1]. Although BreastScreen's recommendations are for women, if you identify with a different gender and have chest/breast tissue you should also follow these screening guidelines. If you have had a mastectomy (removal of chest/breast tissue), then as there is not enough tissue, an x-ray (mammogram) cannot be performed. Other imaging may be used such as ultrasound or magnetic resonance imaging

(MRI), however, unless you are deemed high risk because of a family or personal history of cancer, it is unlikely that this is necessary. If you do not have a high risk of chest/breast cancer, visual inspection and touching your chest (including up to your armpits) to monitor for abnormalities regularly is advised [28-30]. Breast cancer screening in trans women is advised for those aged over 50, who have been on gender-affirming hormonal treatment for more than five years in the form of a mammogram (x-ray of the breast) every two years [28-32]. Breast implants may lower the sensitivity of mammograms, but they have not been linked to an increased risk of breast cancer.

Cancer Screening for Individuals with a Cervix

In Australia, cervical cancer rates have been drastically reduced due to an effective cervical screening program. In fact, one of the biggest risk factors now for developing cervical cancer is lack of attendance to screening services. It is highly important that if you have a cervix, and you have been sexually active in any way, that you have your cervix checked regularly [27].

Please note that the National Cervical Screening Program has changed as of the 1st of December, 2017. Cervical screening is now recommended for individuals with a cervix aged between 25 and 74 every five years. The previous recommendation for cervical screening (Pap smears) was once every two years for people with a cervix aged between 18 and 69. Now, the time between tests is lengthened from two years to five years. Although it is no longer a Pap smear, the test is still performed in a similar way. That is, the healthcare professional needs to take a sample from your cervix, and to do this they have to access your cervix through your frontal opening/vagina. If you find this kind of testing particularly distressing, there are ways it could be made less so:

- Remember that you can say 'stop' at any time.
- You could bring a partner or a friend for support.
- Try relaxation strategies (e.g. music, deep-breathing).

- Talk to your doctor about taking anti-anxiety medication beforehand.
- Tell your healthcare provider what you need them to do – for example to get it over and done with as quickly as possible or do it slowly.
- Discuss with your healthcare provider any problems you may have had in the past.
- Ask for a smaller speculum, more lubricant, or a numbing agent [33, 34].

International research has documented that trans men have a higher rate of 'inadequate Pap smears', and this may extend to other gender diverse individuals with a cervix. An 'inadequate Pap smear' may be due to a variety of factors, and means that the sample taken from the cervix is not able to be tested. It is important, if you have an inadequate test, to return for re-testing within the next few months [35].

Cancer Screening for Individuals with a Prostate

Prostate cancer screening does not have a nation-wide program implemented, and recommendations for prostate cancer screening in cisgender men vary. Prostate cancer is almost exclusively found in people aged over 50, and screening for people at average risk may occur between the ages of 50-69 in the form of a prostate-specific antigen (PSA) test. It is important that healthcare professionals are aware that for trans and gender diverse people on gender-affirming hormone treatment and/or after surgical removal of the gonads/testicles, the PSA level may be lowered. Alternatively, a digital rectal or frontal opening exam may be performed to feel if there are any irregularities [36]. Please remember that most genital surgeries for trans women do not include removal of the prostate. If you have had this surgery, it is still important to pay attention to this body part.

Cancer Screening for Individuals with Ovaries

There is no routine screening for ovarian cancer because there is currently no test that is sensitive enough to be able to diagnose this disease at an early stage. Ovarian cancer has a high mortality rate when diagnosed at a later stage, so it is very important if you notice symptoms associated with ovarian cancer to see your doctor [27]. For people who are concerned about their risk, paying attention to their bodies and having an awareness of the signs and symptoms of ovarian cancer is important. Signs and symptoms may include abdominal pain and bloating, and changes in bowel habits. For individuals who have a family history or genetic susceptibility to ovarian cancer, it may be advisable to have regular pelvic examinations and/or ultrasounds. Please discuss this with your GP or another healthcare provider.

Conclusion

The problems that are posed by the gendering of cancer services for trans and gender diverse people are wide-ranging. Issues exist in relation to discrimination; access to appropriate and sensitive services; lack of research, knowledge and awareness; and the unique needs of this community being unmet. These issues affect all areas of cancer care – risk, screening, diagnosis, treatment, survivorship, and end of life care. There is a critical need for research and health promotion in this complex area, as currently trans and gender diverse people are not receiving equitable cancer care.

References

1.   Cancer Australia, *All Cancers in Australia*, D.o. Health, Editor. 2016, Australian Government: Canberra, ACT.
2.   Bare, M.G., L. Margolies, and U. Boehmer, *Omission of sexual and gender minority patients.* Journal of Clinical Oncology, 2014. **32**(20): p. 2182-2183.
3.   Gooren, L. and P. Lips, *Conjectures concerning cross-sex hormone treatment of aging transsexual persons.* The Journal of Sexual Medicine, 2014. **11**(8): p. 2012-2019.

4. Jones, T. and L. Hillier, *Comparing Trans-Spectrum and Same-sex-Attracted Youth in Australia: Increased Risks, Increased Activisms.* Journal of LGBT Youth, 2013. **10**(4): p. 287-307.

5. Smith, E., et al., *From Blues to Rainbows: Mental health and wellbeing of gender diverse and transgender young people in Australia.* 2014, The Australian Research Centre in Sex, Health and Society, La Trobe University: Melbourne.

6. Taylor, E. and M. Bryson, *Cancer's Margins: Trans* and Gender Nonconforming People's Access to Knowledge, Experiences of Cancer Health, and Decision-Making.* LGBT Health, 2016. **3**(1): p. 79-89.

7. Witten, T. and E. Eyler, *Transgender and Aging: Beings and Becomings*, in *Gay, Lesbian, Bisexual & Transgender Aging: Challenges in Research, Practice & Policy*, T. Witten and E. Eyler, Editors. 2012, John Hopkins University Press: USA.

8. Kumar, V., A. Abbas, and J. Aster, eds. *Robbins and Cotran Pathologic Basis of Disease.* 9 ed. 2015, Saunders, Elsevier Inc.: Canada.

9. Jones, T., et al., *Female-to-Male (FtM) Transgender People's Experiences in Australia: A National Study.* 2015, Switzerland: Springer International Publishing.

10. Couch, M., et al., *TranZnation: A report on the health and wellbeing of transgender people in Australia and New Zealand.* 2007, The Australian Research Centre in Sex, Health and Society, La Trobe University: Melbourne.

11. Boza, C. and K. Nicholson Perry, *Gender-Related Victimisation, Perceived Social Support, and Predictors of Depression Among Transgender Australians.* International Journal of Transgenderism, 2014. **15**(1): p. 35-52.

12. Hyde, Z., et al., *The First Australian National Trans Mental Health Study: Summary of Results.* 2014, School of Public Health, Curtin University: Perth.

13. Riggs, D. and C. Due, *Gender Identity Australia: The healthcare experiences of people whose gender identity differs from that expected of their natally assigned sex.* 2013, School of Social and Policy Studies, Flinders University: Adelaide.

14. Riggs, D., G. Ansara, and G. Treharne, *An Evidence-Based Model for Understanding the Mental Health Experiences of Transgender Australians.* Australian Psychologist, 2015. **59**(1): p. 32-39.

15. McLean, A., *A 'Gender Centre' for Melbourne? Assessing the Need for a Transgender Specific Service Provider.* Gay & Lesbian Issues and Psychology Review, 2011. **7**(1): p. 33-42.

16. Beyond Blue, *In My Shoes: Experiences of discrimination, depression, and anxiety among gay, lesbian, bisexual, trans, and intersex people.* 2012, Beyond Blue: Hawthorn, VIC.

17.   GLBTI Health and Wellbeing Ministerial Advisory Committee, *Transgender and gender diverse health and wellbeing: Background paper.* 2014, Victorian Department of Health: Melbourne.

18.   Winter, S., et al., *Transgender people: health at the margins of society.* The Lancet, 2016. **388**(10042): p. 390-400.

19.   Dresser, R., ed. *Malignant: Medical Ethicists Confront Cancer.* 2012, Oxford University Press: New York.

20.   Brocken, P., et al., *The faster the better?—A systematic review on distress in the diagnostic phase of suspected cancer, and the influence of rapid diagnostic pathways.* Psycho-Oncology, 2012. **21**(1): p. 1-10.

21.   Langhorne, M., J. Fulton, and S. Otto, eds. *Oncology Nursing.* 5 ed. 2007, Mosby Inc.: St. Louis, Missouri.

22.   Trum, H.W., P. Hoebeke, and L.J. Gooren, *Sex reassignment of transsexual people from a gynecologist's and urologist's perspective.* Acta Obstetricia et Gynecologica Scandinavica, 2015. **94**(6): p. 563-567.

23.   Peitzmeier, S., et al., *Pap test use is lower among female-to-male patients than non-transgender women.* American Journal of Preventive Medicine, 2014. **47**(6): p. 808-812.

24.   Power, Jennifer. (2011). *Movement, knowledge, power: Gay activism and HIV/AIDS in Australia.* ANU Press: Canberra.

25.   Burkhalter, J., et al., *The National LGBT Cancer Action Plan: A White Paper of the 2014 National Summit on Cancer in the LGBT Communities.* LGBT Health, 2016. **3**(1): p. 19-31.

26.   Margolies, L. and C. Kamen, *Needs of LGBT Cancer Survivors,* in *Cancer and the LGBT Community: Unique Perspectives from Risk to Survivorship,* U. Boehmer and R. Elk, Editors. 2015, Springer: Switzerland. p. 203-226.

27.   Cancer Council. *Early Detection.* 2017; Available from: http://www.cancer.org.au/about-cancer/early-detection/.

28.   Bond Maycock, L. and H. Powell Kennedy, *Breast Care in the Transgender Individual.* Journal of Midwifery and Women's Health, 2013. **59**(1): p. 74-81.

29.   Phillips, J., et al., *Breast Imaging in the Transgender Patient.* American Journal of Roentgenology, 2014. **202**: p. 1149-1156.

30.   Pivo, S., et al., *Breast Cancer Risk Assessment and Screening in Transgender Patients.* Clinical Breast Cancer, 2016.

31.   Maglione, K.D., et al., *Breast cancer in male-to-female transsexuals: Use of breast imaging for detection.* American Journal of Roentgenology, 2014. **203**(6): p. 735-70.

32.   Weyers, S., et al., *Mammography and breast sonography in transsexual women.* European Journal of Radiology, 2010. **74**(3): p. 508-513.

33.   Bernstein, I., et al., *If You Have It, Check It: Overcoming Barriers to Cervical Cancer Screening with Patients on the Female-to-Male Transgender Spectrum.* 2014, Gay and Lesbian Medical Association: Baltimore.

34.   Potter, J., et al., *Cervical Cancer Screening for Patients on the Female-to-Male Spectrum: a Narrative Review and Guide for Clinicians.* Journal of General Internal Medicine, 2015. **30**(12): p. 1857-1864.

35.   Peitzmeier, S., et al., *Female-to-Male Patients Have High Prevalence of Unsatisfactory Paps Compared to Non-Transgender Females: Implications for Cervical Cancer Screening.* Journal of General Internal Medicine, 2013. **25**(9): p. 778-784.

36.   Weyers, S., et al., *Clinical and transvaginal sonographic evaluation of the prostate in transsexual women.* Urology, 2009. **74**(1): p. 191-196.

Lucille Kerr is a PhD student at La Trobe University, and a Specialist Cancer Nurse. Her current research with Dr Tiffany Jones through ARCSHS is on cancer and the trans and gender diverse community. Data collection will begin in early 2018, and involves surveys to document the patterns of screening in this community as well as the ways the community's strengths can best be utilised in this healthcare area, and one-on-one interviews to explore the experiences of trans and gender diverse individuals who have experienced cancer. Email: L.Kerr@latrobe.edu.au

One Day

SALLY CONNING

I get up around 7 because I don't have to get up for work; except for the weekend when I have to get up at 5:30. I just get up when I want to. I actually make a decision about what the day is going to be. Beside the bed there's always clothes on the floor when I get up; it's always Sally stuff; stuff that makes me feel comfortable, like leg-ins and a dress, or fluffy boots and a big cardigan if it's cold … This morning I put on this long dress and a cardigan.

I go and make a coffee; I have a blue mug that sits on the side of my computer desk; it gets washed once in a while; there's normally a spoon and a bit of coffee still in it …

I'll then fire up the computer and get onto Facebook, mostly reading articles that are trans-related. If there's anything I think is good I'll re-post it …

To me social media is the number one connection for a rural person who has so many friends in the Big Smoke, as I like to call it. I can see what they're doing, they can see what I'm doing, how I'm reacting to things … It gives us a little bit of chit chat that we wouldn't otherwise have, and I'd be, 'What the f*ck am I gonna do now?' By geezus we definitely need social media, and Facebook seems to be it at the moment. Now that we've gotten over the debacle of real names (on Facebook) we're resting easy again …

If I'm not going to work I'll have a shower. Sometimes I put on make-up, sometimes not; sometimes I have my wig on, sometimes not. I get asked if it's really my hair, and I say, 'Yes, I paid for it.'

I then just sit around the house …

That can be typical of six mornings of the week. On Tuesdays and Fridays when I have to go to work, I can feel myself tense slightly, because after my shower I put on work clothes. I used to say I go to work as a guy, I now say I work in guy's clothes, and that's getting harder to do.

My neighbours at the housing commission flats where I live can note the difference in me, because they see both sides of me often …

Getting to work at the servo now is weird; the fact that I'm hiding, I'm hiding the real me… The boss has gotten over my nails; sometimes I'll see him look at my [hairless] arms, his [hairy] arms, and back to my arms; but he doesn't say anything …

My nails seem to be an interesting point at work. I challenged a girl at the servo recently. I gave her back her receipt, and she said, 'Look at your nails, do you play guitar?' I held them up and said, 'Not with these'. She then said, 'That's disgusting!' and walked off. I called after her, 'Why is it disgusting?' Her: 'Because it is …'

Occasionally I'll get asked by women who admit they are jealous and I'll give 'em tips. They ask why I have them and I reply, 'Because I like them.' It's a truthful answer without really saying anything. I'd make a good politician.

Now I just say, 'It's the work clothes'; I go to work, do the hours, have a laugh with the boss, discuss work-related stuff.

My boss is a homophobic, transphobic little sh*t, but a good mate; if you can understand that? The best thing he's said to me is that he'd changed his attitudes towards gay people just a little. It was after Thorpie's coming out interview. He said, 'Good on you Thorpie, I've changed the way I think.' But he's still a homophobic, transphobic little sh*t. [laughs] I know a few trans girls who'll come in sometimes and my boss'll say, 'Get 'em outta the place quick'.

I think about going to work as Sally occasionally, and I think about all the transphobia; it's a suburban petrol station with tradies and older people; two groups that are more likely to be transphobic than others, and so I'll tolerate that until I retire.

At around 4pm if I'm going next door to see my neighbours, I put on some make-up and my 'hat', which is what I sometimes call my wig … Usually I walk in and they'll say, 'Hi Sal' and their little house dog goes nuts. I have free rein of their kitchen, so I'll often make them cups of tea … We tend to like the TV shows, so we'll watch them together. Our favourites change: Midsomer Murders, Frost, typically the English detective shows …

They were there when I moved in here. They're aged pensioners; he's in his 80s, she's mid-70s … I never specifically hid Sally. It was over two years ago, I was going out on a Wednesday night to come up for a night with Seahorse [a Melbourne-based trans support group for almost 40 years]. It was 4:30pm, and both my neighbour and myself were outside. I got in my car. Instead of walking past my car, she walked up. I wound down the window.

Her: 'How's [Sally's boy name]? I haven't seen him in a while, is he OK?'

Sally: 'That's me. I'm [Sally's boy name].'

Her: 'My God you're gorgeous!'

Sally: 'I'll come and have a talk with you about it one day.'

I smiled halfway to Melbourne that night.

Two and a half weeks later I came home from work to check on their dog – they're very particular about their dog – and they invited me in and had a good yak. Ann actually brought up with me about that night and we ended up talking for a good hour and a half. They said, 'It doesn't matter to us'. I said, 'I'll come back one night and you can get to meet Sally properly.'

They were surprised they hadn't seen me previously. When I first started going out, I used to get to the verandah and scamper quickly to the car. Now I walk out, get to the car and think, 'Damn, there's no-one to see me…'

More often than not I'll be invited to stay for dinner; it's a light dinner, which suits me.

I suppose I started really becoming good friends and watching telly with them when my power got cut off. It was during a dispute with the power company. I stopped paying them and decided to bite the bullet; I wanted to see if I could live without power, and found I could which surprised me really …

I was out of the house 6 days of the week and I had gas; a BBQ gas bottle was connected to the house so I could boil my pot of water for my morning coffee. I also found if I put in 2 inches of water in the bathtub and one pot of boiling water I could have a decent wash; I was doing that by candlelight. If I did cook, it was a stewy thing I could heat up in the pot, and I found my old toaster I used when I drove around in my truck. I wasn't watching much television, so I didn't miss much. I guess something I really missed was music.

I like the Rolling Stones, Muse, CCR, AC/DC, Roxy Music, Pink Floyd, I guess anything from the 60s through to current rock, sometimes in the background and sometimes that loud I'm sure the neighbours can hear it …

Every day I would take my laptop next door and charge it up, and that would give me about 4 hours of social media. That was for 58 days and my friendship with my neighbours just grew from there.

I actually rocked up one night recently and knocked on the door, and Ann answered and said, 'Hey Sal,' and leant back and called out to her hubby, 'Hey Roy, it's Sal.' He yelled back, 'Tell her to p*ss off, I want to see him for a change.'

There's occasionally a slip-up, but God, everyone slips up occasionally. After seeing him for 5 years and suddenly there being a she, there's going to be a slip-up with pronouns occasionally; and because they're such supportive friends, I don't care …

Sometimes I'll go to mum's, and I'll say on Facebook, 'My mother's son is going to visit'. Mum's 95, living in a nursing home and being well looked after. When I see her I put on the same pair of slacks and the same shirt; I can remember buying them in the 90s. She loves seeing her son; she's proud of me, in her own way. Over the last few years she's actually started talking to me about Sally in the third person, 'How's

Sally doing?' I put that down to a 95 year old's respect, although she has said to my sister that she does not want to meet me.

I've said to my sister I'll wear those slacks and shirt to my mother's funeral for one last time. That's out of my respect.

Some nights I leave earlier, but tonight's it's 8 o'clock. I'm always told that they love my company, whether it's me, Sally, or it's him. They say they like it that they don't have to put on airs and graces for company …

Tomorrow I'm going to work. At the moment work is a means to an end to get to my retirement. When I get there, I'll retire him completely; I decided that at a Christmas Eve party last year. I'll tolerate the transphobia at work until I retire: 1 year, 8 months and 21 days. I've got my brain so fine-tuned that I can look at the date and know exactly how long it is until I retire. I've never been good at maths, but I know how many days until I retire. It's also a Sunday because I've looked it up.

What am I gonna do on that day? I have no idea … A few girls have a bonfire and burn their boy clothes, but me, it'd only be a small fire … There are already a few people who are lining up to go to my retirement party …

From a collection of interviews and conversations with LGBTIQA+ people across Australia, currently being developed for publication by Daniel Witthaus.

Sally T Conning is a trans elder and sought-after presenter from rural Victoria. She regularly helps train Victoria Police recruits and aged care service providers. Sally is currently writing her own memoir when she's not out and about promoting her #visible365 campaign.

Kneel

BRIGITTE LEWIS

I've knelt down and opened my mouth to check the heart-beat of many
women
it lives there
louder than the organ that sustains us
but only this time have I opened my heart wider than my legs
and said

I love you for the way you make my eyes widen before our lips have a
chance to re-connect
for the spreading you enact across my skin more thorough than the
spread of red across your neck after your first sip of booze no matter
how little you take in
and I know you take it all
I've seen you breathe in the beginnings of words so swiftly my mind
gets whiplash before the space between you having an answer and me
having another question has time to even dance.

And the way you dance is why hips were created
not a swan song to reproduction or biological evolution
but little revolutions
on the dance floor
between our sheets
and the streets we walk

laboured
wide open
and fractured
with the footsteps
we walk across
to find some kind of freedom

hands clasped
fingers bleeding feeling
heads held high
after mornings of crook necks
and outstretched tongues

finding pleasure in each-others' beginnings

this rapture isn't a myth
and I'm not a bone from Adam's rib
I am the end of God's creation
another story to take home
and tell the grandkids I will never have
and the death certificate that will read
unmarried

I love you for the fierce softness that fingers the little bruises under my
chest telling them to heal as you let your desire fire grenades into my
limbs stopping time with every hurricane that rushes over your eyes

a creation story in every kiss
is still more real than the fables
I read when I was in awe of moon face, of fanny
and dick, in the treehouse I always wished existed

but sometimes
everything I ever wanted meets for moments
sometimes days

I have run towards since I believed that dreams could come true
and with you
they do.

with you non-fiction is more beautiful than any story I've read yet.
and I've read so many books my skin has yellowed with the age
of those pages

I still want to yellow
but I want to red, pink, green, and blue with you
I want to red, pink, green, blue, yellow, orange, black, brown and violet
with you.

Brigitte Lewis is a scholarly, literary and poetic writer. She has written on a range of diverse topics including feminisms and feminist digital activisms, lesbian and other types of sex and desire, and cosmopolitanism. She also has skills in the translation of research for mainstream readerships.

The Sticks

DANIEL WITTHAUS

FROM A MEMOIR IN PROGRESS

I learnt the art of a cuppa early. I was a mummy's boy. The thing was, when I hung out with Dad and his mates in the garage; they'd be swigging beer and talking rubbish. Meanwhile Mum was with other women in the kitchen having a cuppa; they'd be telling stories, helping solve each other's problems and gossiping. I knew exactly where I wanted to be. Most of the time I'd sneak in and mum would offer me the last mouthful of her cuppa, which I loved because it was warm and sugary.

These days a cuppa is my simple strategy for social change. In my career I went from working challenging homophobia in schools in Geelong, to flying around the world in developing countries learning about anti-homophobia work. That work that ultimately brought me back to do a 266-consecutive day drive around regional, rural and remote Australia; challenging homophobia one cuppa at a time. I really do believe you can change the world one cuppa at a time. There are many ways a simple cuppa has changed my life… let's share one now and I'll tell you about it.

പ

In December 1996 I first wandered off the streets into the Old Post Office in Geelong, humming, 'I'll tell you what I want, what I really really want', which was the Spice Girls' #1 at the time. I marched seriously up to the large counter and announced to two women that I was there to volunteer with the City of Greater Geelong's gay and lesbian youth support project, GASP. I expected they'd laugh at me and tell me to 'rack off'. To my surprise they invited me back for a trial run. I found out later that Kylie and Leigh were convinced I was only 'volunteering' so that I could score a boyfriend. Six months later I'd have no boyfriend, yet I'd become a part of the furniture.

Back then there was no Australian research, but every single young person I came across, without fail, described school as shit or crap. This was back in the days where it was almost impossible and virtually unheard of for any work to happen in schools. When I asked the major LGBTI organisations for help, I was laughed at and told to 'rack off'. A gay man running one major organisation told me I was pushing shit up hill, and, 'If it's so bad, why don't you just move to Melbourne?' A lesbian academic warned me, 'If you try, you're going to fuck it up for a generation of young people,' and, besides, 'They'd never let YOU into a school, and a Catholic school, forget it!'

I went back to Geelong with the wind knocked out of my sails. But I got sick of saying to young people, 'Fingers crossed you have a better week at school this week'. So I had cuppas with every local teacher and worker I could.

I was told in 1997 to wait for the education department to implement policy. They would do so, 11 years later. I was told to wait for an inclusive sexual health resource called Catching On. It caught on 7 years later. Long before Safe Schools was hailed as a 'first' in school curriculum in 2010, Safe *In* Schools was funded and rolled out in Victorian schools by Family Planning Victoria, in 2003. In 1997 I was told to wait for more experienced workers to find a solution, but the young people I worked with didn't have the luxury of time. So I decided not to wait.

◌

One of the first schools I worked in as a youth worker was one of the roughest in Geelong. I remember one Friday afternoon we were in the school hall working with 30 of the toughest boys on an arts and footy project. And that's typical Geelong; trust everything to revolve around football (and don't get me started on Bollards). It was strange because everyone was quiet and working on various tasks, and that NEVER happened.

I knew exactly why. Earlier that week I'd done a talk about gay people in the Year 10 Health class. After the first class, the news spread around the school in about 1.7 seconds. Soon a group of loiterers gathered at the door to look in through the window. One of them was a year nine student called Tim. Tim was pacing the floorboards, eyes fixated on his feet and mumbling to himself. A crowd gathered; he became louder. Some students were confused; some were laughing. Tim stepped in and said, 'Are you gay?'

It might seem strange: but I hadn't prepared myself for that question; you have to remember this was back when you could lose your job for revealing something like that. I had a split second to think: I'd earned their trust and respect over the last few months, I wasn't gonna lie now. I had no idea what would happen, but I gave the only answer I could: YES.

Pete, one of two alpha males for the group stepped in.

Pete: So f**king what if Danza is gay Tim?

Tim: Oh, I don't know. I just don't know what I'm supposed to think about it.

Pete: Who gives a sh*t d*ckhead?

As quickly as it happened, it all ended.

Three Fridays later the two alpha males of the group, Pete and Joe, made their way towards me. Now I'd watched a lot of *Prisoner* growing up, and I knew the 'Top Dog' was gonna talk, and I had to listen. I also thought about how Joe had been suspended recently for punching a teacher in the head and breaking his nose. They shuffled shoulder-to-shoulder, closer and closer to me, and EVERY set of eyes in the hall were on us.

Pete: Danza, um …

Joe: We've got something to say, Danza …

Me: OK guys, I'm all ears …

Pete: Well Danza, you have to know … That we… Um, that we hate faggots right …?

Joe: Yeah, we hate faggots …

Pete: Shut up dickhead and let me finish!

Joe: OK, fucken hurry up then!

Pete: We hate faggots Danza … But you're OK …

At that point both broke out into cheeky grins from ear to ear. I'd never seen them look so proud of themselves. Each shook my hand in turn, *firmly*.

Me: Thanks guys …

Over the next few months I witnessed the group's homophobic language and behaviour reduce to almost zero. Whilst funny for a few weeks, 'we hate faggots but you're OK', was something I'd challenge; if they could get along with one, then maybe they could get along with more. And whilst we're at it, we're coming up with another word for gay people, OK? The accidental lesson would form the basis of my future challenging homophobia work in schools: *Pride & Prejudice*.

℗

I never planned to go into an all-boys Catholic school. I was 21 the day I drove to St Regional College as a young gay atheist. I walked through the school grounds, which were perfect and green, and the buildings were old and made of bluestone; nothing like my own school years (portable classrooms and a dry, grassless oval). I'd actually come prepared for a low-expectation cuppa with the School Welfare Coordinator, Maude, but as soon as I arrived, she said, 'Oh, and could I get you a tea or coffee before I go? You'll be meeting with the Deputy Principal …'

After Maude left, even if I was an atheist, I prayed to God that Maude would return first. Not so. In walked Ross, one of the most imposing men I'd ever seen. He seemed seven foot tall. Thus, I proved that God doesn't exist. Ross extended a hand; I shook it nervously.

Maude soon returned with a cup of black tea with two sugars before excusing herself. But maybe there is a God and she smiled down that day, for Ross wanted to hear more about how we could work together. Not only was he personally and professionally motivated to do something, he explained how the staff at his school had extra motivation. A former student, let's call him Ben, had written to St Regional recently. The following letter was read out at a staff meeting:

> To whom it may concern,
>
> I felt the need to write after receiving the latest edition of the 'Old Boys' Newsletter. Rather than joy, I was filled with dread even before I opened it.
>
> Although I left St Regional College 10 years ago, this newsletter brought back all the things I experienced when I was a student. Being gay meant I was bullied by students and teachers alike; they made my life a living hell.
>
> Not only does it upset me every time I think about St Regional College, it also makes me think about what life might be like for current students who are gay. I can only hope they don't experience what I did.
>
> I ask you to kindly stop sending me correspondence from St Regional College. I don't want to hear about what any other student is doing now, or reminisce about the old times.
>
> I'm sorry but I don't want to be reminded that the school exists.
>
> Yours, Ben.

The teacher who read the letter had wept. To end our meeting, Ross leaned forward, 'I wonder Daniel, how comfortable are you talking in front of large groups? Because – before you answer – I've got 75 Catholic school teachers that I'd like you to talk to.'

What many people don't know about me is that I'm an introvert … an introvert from a family of extroverts. My older brother played sports and was the toughest kid in the Bronx; my sister was into netball and very social. I just wanted to read the atlas, study the Solar System and play with Lego (and my He-man figures and Transformers). I hadn't ever wanted to stand up and talk in front of groups, but now I found a reason. I realised that if I didn't go and do the gay talks in local schools or speak to those 75 Catholic school teachers, then no-one would. Were there more qualified, experienced people in Geelong who could speak up for LGBTI young people? Yes. Were they likely to do so anytime soon? No, and some told me so. Did I want to be that person? No.

Without overstating it, I had two choices: on the one hand were local young LGBTI people and what they were facing in schools; on the other I had my own self-doubt and insecurities. Who was I to do nothing, and what made my needs more important than theirs? So keeping in mind I had zero experience, and that the thought of public speaking made me want to vomit, my answer still doesn't make sense.

'Yes Ross, I'll talk to your staff.'

It went OK, otherwise I wouldn't be here today. But the aftermath … In modern times where things have moved so much, it's hard to describe how bananas people went; teachers from schools I'd never heard of, media outlets targeting young people, youth workers, gay and lesbian people. There were all of these things that didn't go together: challenging homophobia, all-boys Catholic schools, year nine students, then-Archbishop George Pell and regional Australia. In reality, no-one could blame me if it didn't work. Yet it did. It surprised me as much as anyone.

Suddenly I was being invited into other schools, presenting at conferences and talking to the media. It went viral before things really went viral. At first it was a dream come true. Then by the fifth school, I had a problem. I realised I couldn't get to every school and that change could only occur if teachers *everywhere* were delivering challenging homophobia content themselves.

Not that I knew what to do about it, until one day I took questions at a conference in Ballarat. A woman near the back, with unusually big hair leant forward and said, 'Oh, you gay people …' Everyone turned and waited for what would come out of her mouth.

Her: Oh you gay people, if only you realised that we'd do this if you put it into a package for us teachers…

Me: Tell me more…

Her: Well if you had all the session plans, the handouts and a video – kids love videos these days – and you put it all into a folder, then we'd run it…

Me: You're serious? All it'd take would be to do that?

Her: Of course. I'd run it if you did that …

Two years later, in 2002, I launched *Pride & Prejudice* in partnership with Deakin University and VicHealth; a six-week, step-by-step guide for teachers who wanted to challenge homophobia and support students in everyday classrooms. Deakin University found such challenging homophobia work can significantly improve student attitudes towards gay men and lesbians and may reduce 'homo-aggressive' behaviour.

℃

There've been plenty of times when I've seriously contemplated giving up. But I'll let you in on a secret: the reason I keep going is quite simple; the seed was planted when I was about 11 years of age.

It was one Sunday, late in the morning when dad yelled 'Daniel Edward!' which meant I needed to get to the living room. I found dad standing and staring out the window, which was unusual because he was always sitting in his chair reading a book. Bob Dylan was blasting from his reel-to-reel and he motioned for me to join him.

I stood beside him and he put an arm around my shoulders, grabbing me firmly.

'I want you to listen to this next song, this is important. I want it played at my funeral.'

He looked down at me.

'Do you understand? This song is to be played at my funeral.'

I nodded.

At that point in my life no-one had died, so the thought of my strong, reliable father dying freaked me out. I stood staring out the window, feeling awkward; he seemed completely comfortable. With roast lamb and vegetables wafting from the kitchen I stood and wondered why he'd picked me for such an important piece of information.

I then listened as the next song started – a song I'd never heard before: 'Desolation Row'.

It starts: 'They're selling postcards of the hanging, they're painting the passports brown, the beauty parlour is filled with sailors, the circus is in town.'

This is all fine until you realise that 'Desolation Row' goes for 11 minutes and 21 seconds.

Being a rare bootleg album, it meant I'd never hear it again.

In my 20s I had a habit of looking for Bob Dylan CDs every time I was near a record/CD shop (remember those?). I'd look at the song listing, and never once did I find 'Desolation Row'.

It wasn't until the internet allowed for the 'downloading' of music that I finally found it. I was reluctant at first, but listened to it over and over again for months. I listened to the lyrics, yet it didn't really sink in.

Then one night in Berlin, alone in a friend's penthouse, I actually 'heard' the final verse. Suddenly it all made sense; the reason my dad wanted it played at his funeral was so that he could have the last laugh. In the final verse Dylan gives everyone he knows a backhander, after fooling them with a distracting performance.

I thought of my dad's life, the people who surrounded him and his mutterings to me over the years; there was honestly no-one around him that he liked or respected. Once he was dead, he could reveal his utter contempt for the world and everyone in it, especially those around him. He knew that most people wouldn't get it; he thinks everyone else is stupid, and his intelligence is superior.

If I'm honest with myself, I see that potential in me; that ability to easily hate the world and everyone in it, and to want to shut myself away. And I'm shit scared I'll become just like him: smiling and jovial on the outside; full of venom on the inside. It's no way to live a life.

છ

As a youth worker I speak to so many people who want to support rural LGBTI people, especially young people. Yet they feel overwhelmed, like it's too impossible to do anything about it. Let me assure you, there's plenty we can all do, one cuppa and chat at a time, especially in rural and remote areas. In truth, there's never been a better time to be L, G, B, T or I in this country … unless you're not linked in and supported, in which case your experience could be what it was 15-20 years ago.

A young man once described homophobia to me as the proverbial death of a thousand cuts. It's not one incident that does you in, it's the accumulation of small hurts over time. For me, community is an accumulation of small kindnesses over time from those around us that negate those small hurts. We can all do something about that, however small, and often just by reaching out to people over a cuppa and a chat. Getting this right is too important. Young LGBTIs in rural areas want to live in an Australia where they can simply be themselves and hold the hand of the person they love without fear or concern for their safety. For most, they don't yet live in that Australia.

Daniel Witthaus has spent over two decades challenging homophobia 'one cuppa at a time' in schools, rural communities and, occasionally, developing countries like Sri Lanka, Poland and Indonesia. He is the author of *Beyond Priscilla: one gay man, one gay truck, one big idea...* (2014), *Beyond 'That's So Gay!': Challenging homophobia in Australian schools* (2010) and the *Pride & Prejudice* educational package (2002, 2012). In 2013 Daniel founded the National Institute for Challenging Homophobia Education (NICHE), which focuses on the needs of LGBTI people in regional, rural and remote Australia. www.niche.org.au.

Distance/ Love/Guns

MIRA SCHLOSBERG

In the afternoons we wait outside school together. Tall tall ponderosa pines swaying, heavy rushing sound of wind through pine needles. We speak very little, just stand next to each other.

The only time I go to her house is when we are fifteen, before a school dance. Week-old patches of ice greying at the edges of her driveway. I sit in the corner reading *Seventeen* while all the other girls do each other's hair. She is wearing her pyjamas, the waistband is slipping down and I can see she has on ruffly red underwear. Two of our friends spent the previous night here. I think about them sleeping in her bed. She has a pet cockatoo and it is screaming downstairs like it's being murdered. The screaming is making her two dogs go skittering in and out of the room again and again.

In *Seventeen* there is an article called 'My Boyfriend Turned out to be a Girl'. One of those it-happened-to-me sort of articles. The boyfriend in question has disappeared after having his secret revealed. The girlfriend is devastated. I loved him, she says. It wouldn't have mattered to me if he just told me the truth.

I carpool to school with a boy who, at sixteen, is strongly self-identified as a Libertarian. He annotates the summer history reading with convoluted arguments against it. His politics are a school-wide joke, but a friendly one.

A lot of the boys at school have guns, for weekend hunting trips with their dads. In Arizona you don't need a permit to purchase a firearm, and it is legal for minors to carry a loaded gun if they are accompanied by a guardian. There is a push in the state government to lift the ban on concealed firearms on university campuses, and for a while this discussion sometimes includes elementary and high schools as well. The teachers laugh and say that the boy I carpool with is the one most likely to start bringing a gun to class. Are you packing heat right now, says our history teacher, where do you normally keep your guns? He says he keeps them locked in a box at home for safety, but he doesn't answer when the teacher asks if he ever carries a gun outside of school.

There are not a lot of good options for prom dates junior year. She asks him to take her, and he says yes, but he has a shift at work that night so he will be late. We go to dinner in a big group and she sits next to me. We have matching tulle skirts. We dance together. He shows up sometime later. I think, at least he brought her a corsage.

My boyfriend throws me a surprise party for my birthday and she is there. I haven't seen her all summer. There is a meteor shower going on and we go outside to see it. I lay next to her on the driveway. The concrete is still hot from the sun. Smell of dusty desert air. We see a meteor falling, a pink streak in the sky.

In January of our senior year, the Arizona State Representative Gabrielle Giffords is shot in the head in a Safeway parking lot. Four months later Arizona becomes the second state in the US to approve legislation designating an official state firearm. The chosen gun is the Colt Single Action Army Revolver, known as the Peacemaker.

We have given up trying to get prom dates. She lives near me; I ask her for a ride. She shows up at my door in a purple and teal satin gown, her chest all encrusted with jewels, freckled shoulders bare. My mother takes photos of us in front of her Volkswagen beetle.

After the dance she drives me home again. We sit in her car for a moment, saying goodbye. I thank her for the ride. I imagine us leaning towards each other over the stick shift and kissing. I get out of the car and walk around it towards my building, and then I open the driver's side door and say by the way you looked really good tonight. She says thanks, you looked beautiful too.

At graduation I am given a yellow rose. She says she loves the colour and I say here you can have it. In two days I am moving to Sydney with my family, and at the end of the summer she is going to McGill in Montreal.

In Sydney the wattles bloom huge furry clouds of yellow blossoms. They fill the air and cover the sidewalk outside my house like our favourite scene in *One Hundred Years of Solitude*. I write to her about the wattles. She writes to me about pastries. I send her a pressed jacaranda flower. She sends me snowflakes melted on the page, still smelling wet and cold. I tell her I have a girlfriend. She doesn't mention it in her reply.

Sometimes I think about us as something running parallel to my real life. She is so far away, and we don't talk except in letters, and in short Facebook messages confirming that letters have been sent or received. In high school I was convinced we were connected by some kind of psychic bond, that we didn't need to discuss our importance to each other because it was something we both just knew. I don't believe this anymore, but there are ways to express love without stating it directly. We are experts at this.

It's four years before I tell her how I used to feel. Past tense. How I wanted to kiss her at prom. She says she remembers that moment and that she wanted it too.

In June of 2015 the United States Supreme Court declares same-sex marriage legal in all fifty states. Somewhere online I read that, historically, advancements like this in civil rights are always followed by conservative retaliation. Visibility leads to violence. Scrolling through Twitter becomes a surreal experience. Sometimes a queer person's selfie is just a selfie, and sometimes it is accompanied by an article about another suicide, or a murder.

At the start of 2016 I move to Melbourne, change my pronouns. I stand at the same bus stop every day watching the sun on the leaves of a eucalyptus tree. In April my cousin gets (straight) married in Santa Cruz. I fly into SFX and my parents pick me up in a rental car and drive me back along the coast. It's the first time I've been back to the U.S. since I left. We stop at Half Moon Bay, low hills all around, green scrub with purple flowers growing in the sand on the beach. All space and light and the sound of wind. I put my feet in the ocean.

She is living in San Diego and she drives up to see me. She is taller than I remember and her voice sounds like I have never heard it before, but otherwise she seems exactly the same. We drive towards the water, find a dog beach. It is a thin strip below some rocks and there are dogs running all over it, wet and caked in sand. We have one towel and we lay it on the ground in the tiny patch of shade up against the rocks. When I sit down I lean back on the arm that is closest to her, so that if we were inches closer my arm would be around her.

We are too close to the water and before we have been sitting there even a minute a wave creeps up and suddenly there is water all around us and our shoes are floating away. I jump up and run after my boots. I can hear her behind me shrieking.

We rescue our things from the ocean and retreat to higher ground. The towel is saturated with seawater and we heave it onto a concrete wall to dry. I watch her wringing water from her skirt.

I have planned what to say but I am not saying it. Standing almost too close to her feels natural, but to swing an arm up and touch her shoulder, or pull her close to me, would be impossible. I am too queer now, too butch for a soft girl. My hands are coated in wet sand and I wipe them on my pants. They hang clean at my sides for a minute, and then I grab the corner of the towel and twist it. Water runs down my wrists until my hands are all gritty again. The sun feels warm all over my body and then, at the back of my neck, too hot like it is starting to burn.

We climb back up to the path above the beach and cross the street to a patch of long grass. We sit on a stump under a tree and talk about how things are different. We both have tattoos now. She lifts up her shirt to show me the cherry blossoms on her ribs.

I am watching a bird in the grass. When it flies away I will ask her. I am counting my breaths. I will take three more and then ask her. A lot of birds come and go. I breathe very slowly for a long time.

I say do you want to kiss, you know, to make up for prom. She says I think so. I figure it will be quick and then it will be over, but instead the kiss starts and it doesn't stop. My eyes are closed but I am thinking about the freckles at the tops of her cheekbones and I touch her hair and her arms are around me and it is a sad kiss but a good one. Finally a truck pulls up behind us and a bunch of men are shouting at us and we turn around and stare at them until they drive away.

When we walk back along the cliff she asks to hold my hand and I ask her if it is ok to do that here. She says she thinks so. There is no one around except a middle-aged couple further up the path. We hold hands and when we walk past the couple the woman stares.

I had been afraid that seeing her again would be too much. That if we kissed it would become obvious that we had to be together and I would have to drop out of school and move back to the states for good. But when she leaves I feel ok. We have lived on different continents for five years now. It seems unimportant that we might not see each other for another five. It isn't until the next day that I cry about it.

In June I am at home, lying in bed at night and cycling aimlessly through social media apps when I start seeing tweets about a mass shooting in the U.S. At first I scroll past; it's not out of the ordinary. But after an hour or so there are hardly any tweets about anything else. I read that nearly fifty people have died in a gay club in Florida, that it is one of the biggest shootings ever to happen in the United States.

In the morning social media is flooded with people talking about Orlando. I feel strange, afraid of something that is so far away now. A threat that is hazy but so familiar. There are things about the way I look that mean I am less at risk than others, but I still don't feel safe.

I have to go to the office of the magazine I work for to help proofread the new issue. We talk about page numbers and how to spell the authors' names correctly. It is the weekend and we are the only ones in the building. It is quiet and familiar, but there are so many of us that the work takes hardly any time at all, and soon I am waiting for the train home and reading Twitter again. I want to go back to the office and lie on the floor between the desks and not be alone. I think about messaging the editor to ask if there is anything else I can help with, but then the train comes and I get on it. All the Australians on Twitter are talking about how strange and horrific a shooting is. It takes me a minute to register why they are so surprised. I think about the boy from my carpool and the locked box of guns in his house. I think about how the teachers laughed at him, and how I know that now he is teaching history at that same school. A few rows in front of me a guy and a girl are cuddled up together. He has his arm around her and their heads are resting against each other. I am crying and the woman across from me is trying not to look at me.

I get off the train and onto the bus. By the furniture warehouse a few stops from my house I pull my phone from my pocket again. I scroll back to our last messages, from April. It was nice seeing you, I'll miss you, etc. I type a new one. I hope you are ok, I say. I love you. She writes back thank you. I am ok despite the tragedy. I love you too.

———————————

Mira Schlosberg is a writer, editor and comics artist whose work has been published in *The Lifted Brow*, *Seizure*, and *Scum Mag*, among others. You can find Mira on Twitter @miraschlosberg.

History, Glitter, Skulls

DANIEL MARSHALL

Taylor Mac at the Melbourne Festival

October was a strange month, a ghost of a month. The same sex marriage survey and so much of what went with it gave a toxic atmosphere to so much of everything. I had organized an event for Queer History Month early in October, but my Mum got sick and had to be admitted to hospital quite suddenly, so we had to cancel. Months earlier I'd bought tickets for the two of us to see Taylor Mac's *24-Decade History of Popular Music* at the Melbourne Festival, but she was not well enough to go.[1] As the month went on, she improved, and so my routine, for a few days at least, became days in the hospital, then nights at Melbourne's Forum theatre for Mac's show, twenty-four hours over four nights. The hospital and the theatre are both their own types of

---

[1] Conceived as a 24-hour performance tracing American history through 24 years of music popular in the United States, the show was performed in four chapters of six hours over four nights: Chapter One: 1776—1836; Chapter Two: 1836—1896; Chapter Three: 1896—1956; and Chapter Four: 1956—present (https://www.festival.melbourne/2017/events/a-24-decade-history-of-popular-music/#.WfbQ5610ii4). Also see: http://stannswarehouse.org/show/taylor-mac-24-decade-history-popular-music-1776-2016/

grieving place – cordoned-off spaces, spaces where you can find yourself with strangers, spaces where you can slip away. Like churches, they are spaces full of ghosts; you can see them out dancing in front of you. Moving between those strange spaces of hospital and theatre, with the big mess of survey feelings hanging over my head, I felt a bit out of focus, like the ghosting you sometimes get in the static on TV. Unhappy with all the survey mess, I just wanted the times to be different, and for 24 hours, with Taylor Mac, they were.

A Long Way from the Farm

I first saw Taylor Mac perform at the Lincoln Centre in 2014 when I was in New York on sabbatical. It was a riotous, bracing, joyful experience. I had gone to the show with a friend and we had unwittingly bought fancy tickets so we were sitting at this little round table just in front of the stage with a complimentary bottle of wine on it, and the glittering Manhattan skyline providing a dramatic backdrop behind the stage. I was a kid who had grown up on a farm in Glencoe, a tiny South Australian town with two shops and more churches. A James Bond movie marathon on television was a cultural event. So, the glamour of this New York experience was overwhelming and otherworldly. It was a long way from the farm.

Mac was performing a decade – the 1920s – from the larger work, *A 24-Decade History of Popular Music*. In Mac's telling of it, the 1920s becomes less a story about post-war euphoria and heterosexual romance and more a love story about Larry and Barry and post-traumatic stress disorder in the wake of the slaughter of World War I.[2] In Mac's telling, we are invited to observe how queerness is often suppressed in historical reflections on people's intimate lives and how trauma often gets suppressed by celebrations of nationalism and profit. Narration circulates as a key idea or problematic in Mac's work: who gets to speak and who doesn't? How is the story structured? What kinds of characters are typically used to tell a story, and in what typical ways?

---

[2] http://www.womanaroundtown.com/sections/playing-around/taylor-macs-24-decade-history-of-popular-music-the-1920s-uptown-and-inside

Who gets left out? What might be some new ways of telling stories about familiar things? Indeed, Mac describes Mac's role as the role of narrator.[3] This desire to make apparently familiar stories strange, to contest established historical narratives and crack them open to find difference inside, was played out across the stage at the Lincoln Centre that night. In Mac's hands, history, far from being a settled story, is ripped open and made ready for the telling again.

And the telling requires labour, so Mac places particular demands on the audience. As Mac is a 'reminder', not a teacher, active participation of the audience is required. Mac convenes an audience, which is then invited to participate in a variety of ways, usually as characters. By providing narrative information throughout the performance, Mac characterizes, frames and sequences moments of performance that the audience is asked to help make happen. The audience participation is rationalized in implicit and explicit ways. First, Mac's shows are about performing history as a way of demonstrating that history should not be removed from experience, but is produced by experience. Audience participation in the performance of history is not supplemental in these shows but essential because Mac is reminding us that histories ought to be of the people, and that it is in people's histories that we can find alternative stories which can challenge and replace the exclusions and hierarchical values of those histories narrated at one remove (this emphasis on people's histories is also demonstrated by the focus in the show on popular music as a widely accessible art form).[4] Secondly, by expecting the audience to participate in the performance of the historical, Mac invites the audience to get a feeling for how historical stories get stitched together, to get up close to see narrative at work, and to think, then, on some other perspectives, some other ways of telling the story.

As part of this work of re-narrating history as stories of often neglected others, Mac asks the audience to experience discomfort, and, as Mac makes clear, the audience participation in Mac's work is employed as a key way of producing this discomfort. Needless to say,

---

[3] 'In Conversation' event, Melbourne.
[4] 'In Conversation' event, Melbourne.

not all audience participation discomfort is equal – a man proudly sharing a personal story about sex and vomit is quite different to being called up on stage and told to impersonate a Nazi, for example.[5] Experiences of discomfort can resonate in complex ways, and this unpredictability demands a critical attentiveness. Often, Mac interrupts audience pleasure to remind us to come back to our critical attentiveness, prompting us to reflect on questions like, why am I laughing at that? Why do I just want to sing along to the song I know? Discomfort in its many forms is worked as a technique to push us beyond what we are comfortable with as part of an approach to clear away some space to make room for thinking about things from a different vantage point. Mac is serious when describing the *24 Hour* show as a 'radical faerie realness ritual sacrifice'[6], in which 'the audience is the sacrifice'.[7] The show asks that you give something, and its length and durational structure is only the most explicit signpost of this to the audience in a show ripe with invitations to give.

These twin techniques – the defamiliarization or ripping open of history, and the use of discomfort to problematize positionality and inherited knowledge – hit me full in the face as Mac took to the stage that night in New York, belting out 'Happy Days Are Here Again!'. Mac joked that to recreate the pervasive trauma characterizing the post-WW1 experience, we could just sing that song on a manic loop for the hour. This joke about repetition and re-enactment reminds us how such exaggerated reiteration can help us to see a familiar thing anew. Through repetition, the substance of the thing gets distorted and its integrity starts to warp. In a room full of replicas, the way you see the original changes (the Cast Courts in London offer another example in a

---

[5] These are examples taken from the 2017 Melbourne Festival performances of the *24 Decade* show and *The Inauguration*, respectively.
[6] http://sometimesmelbourne.blogspot.com.au/2017/10/; also see https://theatrepress.com.au/2017/10/08/melbourne-festival-2017-the-inauguration-with-taylor-mac/
[7] http://www.smh.com.au/entertainment/stage/melbourne-stage/almost-a-religious-experience-taylor-mac-opus-leaves-audience-weeping-for-more-20171021-gz5k07.html

different artistic context[8]). Through repetition and re-enactment in the *24 Decade* show, the original thing – a version of history that effaces difference, for example – warps and distorts through exaggerations and interruptions, and begins to fall apart. Attention shifts to all the broken pieces as the most tangible evidence of what remains, and what can be built from them. If memory serves, Mac's collaborator, Machine Dazzle, had created a boa out of loaves of sliced white bread as part of Mac's elaborate costume for the New York performance that night (sliced white bread, we were informed, became a thing in the 1920s). And, as Mac, energetically moved through the audience, singing and dancing through the crowd, the 'loaf-of-bread boa'[9] gradually began to fall apart, leaving breadcrumbs here and there (or is that my imagination?). In the songs, the script, the costumes, the set we found cues and clues of histories that were called up as if for some kind of exorcism: there are ghosts here![10] The past is not settled! Falling apart, the costume leaves a trail of histories: queer histories and breadcrumbs, a fairy tale path to follow. And where is it taking us?

Mac describes *A 24-Decade History of Popular Music* as 'a 24-hour music theater work about how communities are built as a result of being torn apart.'[11] When I went to the New York show, I had been spending a lot of time thinking about fragments and crumbs as metaphors of queer history, of how queer history as a body of knowledge was built from scarcity and violence by communities under pressure 'of being torn apart.'[12] What are the implications of living with a history that is built from rubble, even while a lot of glitter runs

---

[8] http://www.vam.ac.uk/content/articles/t/the-cast-courts/
[9] http://www.womanaroundtown.com/sections/playing-around/taylor-macs-24-decade-history-of-popular-music-the-1920s-uptown-and-inside
[10] For another discussion of the show and ghosts please see: https://www.nytimes.com/2016/10/11/theater/review-taylor-macs-24-hour-concert-was-one-of-the-great-experiences-of-my-life.html
[11] http://www.taylormac.org/portfolio_page/24-decade/
[12] http://www.taylormac.org/portfolio_page/24-decade/

through it?[13] And history relentlessly grows: since Gay Liberation, our knowledge of queer history has expanded on a massive scale. And accompanying this inheritance is also the historical knowledge about how previous generations of people excavated and made available queer historical scholarship. Histories of queers, and histories of people writing histories of queers. All of the histories begin to pile up: fragments, crumbs, rubble. I became preoccupied with metaphors of accretion and layering, about how building a shared understanding of queer life was a project of somehow carrying these fragments, of feeling them as they all kept piling up. It is almost too much history for one body to bear; it is a history that demands many bodies, a people's history. On stage, that night at the Lincoln Centre, I saw a performer who seemed to feel the weight of this queer history, and to carry it defiantly, both as an act of celebration and as an act of demanding ongoing critical reflection. Taylor Mac made me feel like there were, if we all tried hard enough, just enough bodies in that theatre to bear just enough of the histories we have to carry. It felt like a moment where queer history, as fragmentary and problematic as much of it is, was lifted up and turned into some kind of fierce, collective live action abundance. I have not had ECT, but Mac does love metaphors, and so I felt on that night that I was having some kind of queer history shock therapy; I was electrified by it. *I mean, I even wrote Taylor a fucking fan letter,* and I don't think I've ever done that before. So, when I found out Mac was coming to Melbourne, I got tickets for everything I could.

24 Hours

Experiencing the show in Melbourne was an overwhelming experience – the sheer scale of the show is hard to fathom, there is so much detail, so much beauty and wit and musical and visual sophistication that writing about it yields only fragmentary recollections. I guess I am writing them down now as a way of trying to keep hold of some of

---

[13] For another discussion of rubble please see Edgecomb, Sean F. (2017) 'A Review of Taylor Mac's 24-Decade History of Popular Music Marathon,' *PARtake: e Journal of Performance as Research*: Vol. 1 : Iss. 2 , Article 10.

them. Maybe because I was exhausted from the hospital I didn't take down notes through the performance or take photos. I just let it wash over me, like a tide coming in. Live performance as a wave, history as a wave: there is so much, and then it is gone. So, I am not sure how reliable my account of the performances is, and quotes that I attribute to others are taken from memory; apologies for any errors. This is also only a discussion of a few parts of the show; there is so much more to say.

The excitement or anxiety of live theatre or music is the knowledge that the ephemeral live moment is lost. And, because there is so much in this show, there is so much to lose. But the *24 Decade* show makes living with loss a central concern, specifically because it is a show built around remembering so many things that they pile up beyond capacity. Mac talks about how the length of the show is designed, in part, to produce the experience of things falling apart: 'I want the show to be so long that the audience is falling apart, I'm falling apart, we're all falling apart and we're also building bonds'.[14] The durational structure of the show reminds us how the act of remembering is always bound to failure; how remembering is important not only because of what it preserves but of how it also teaches us to live with loss, and what the implications are when you confront the reality that you can't necessarily repair things, can't put all the pieces back together again. And yet, from start to finish, the show is not about promoting a fragmented experience but one in which people are brought together through experiences of loss and failure, a show that, in the end, takes metaphors of fragments and brokenness and knits them together into a new experience of wholeness (and yes, I use 'knitting' here on purpose, recalling the knitters on stage before the show began, metaphors of creation, as Mac explained it). And so, I think one of the powerful provocations of this show is that it asks us to trouble our ready reliance on brokenness as a metaphor for history and for life. I think it

---

[14] https://www.theguardian.com/stage/2017/sep/13/taylor-mac-on-queering-history-someone-like-me-doesnt-normally-get-to-represent-america

challenges us to reflect on the question: have we become comfortable thinking in fragments?

'Amazing Grace' or 'Perfection is for Assholes'

To open the *24 Decade* show, Mac walks through the audience singing 'Amazing Grace'. This sets the terms for the entire show, following its narrative arc through 240 years of American history. It is an enduring question: what is grace? Might it be that quality that is found in living with brokenness, in living with the rubble on your back? Mac again and again opens up the performance as a space for doing the living that happens in imperfect ways. By declaring, 'Perfection is for assholes!' as a motto for the show, Mac invites the audience in, encouraging us to sing along even when we don't know the words, or participate even when we don't or can't follow the instructions properly. Grace might be that experience of the intimacy of imperfection, of trying though failing, and through such failure, realizing the precarity of our bonds with others, the world, and sometimes our sense of ourselves.

In the *24 Decade* show, intimacy is produced, in part, by Mac's efforts to guide us to see how we are all in this (the performance, history, the social) together. But early on Mac issued a cautionary note: 'We are in mixed company', so some things might get misunderstood. This was a queer performance, Mac went on, but not a performance of the queer performer as exotic spectacle. By expressing the point that the performers are not 'freaks for spectators' (or words to that effect) but 'freaks' for the purposes of eroding social conventions, of pointing to the silliness of so many conventions, and of helping to encourage us all into queerness – describing us all as being 'minions of the spirit of dandy now' (or words to that effect) – Mac calls on all of us to take up a role in the reinvestigation of history playing out on stage. 'It's not a universal show,' Mac says, criticizing the notion that people go to the theatre only to see reflections of themselves. But its resonances are profound, with the show occasionally making explicit reference to Australian histories. After a statue of Governor Macquarie is torn down on stage, Mac puts it simply saying that: 'you think you don't have a white supremacy problem here, but you do' (or words to that effect).[15]

The first chapter closes with a critique of the racism of colonialism in historical narrative. Ending with a story about an indigenous woman breaking free from the colonisers, Mac presents her as also eventually evading the story that Mac wants to tell about her. As the chapter comes to a close on the thematics of indigenous vengeance ('By the banks of the Ohio'), the indigenous woman ruptures the narrative and changes her name – she is, I think, 'Ellipsis' now. Life after colonialism can't be reassembled the way it was before the boats from Europe arrived, but that does not mean that indigenous people can only be known in ways that conform with how non-indigenous people want to tell stories about these things. The future is unwritten, elliptical.

Against 'Cheap Sentiment'

Chapter two extends the focus on the politics of race through a staged 'battle' between 'abolitionist songs by ineffective white liberal' (or words to that effect) and songs of resistance sung by slaves themselves. A focus in this chapter is on the ways that oppressors used popular songs to make themselves feel better about things like dispossessing indigenous people, owning people and profiting from an unfair class system. (Throughout the show, Mac's beautiful performances of songs like 'Hard Times' and, later, Woody Guthrie's 'Dust Can't Kill Me', underline a class consciousness which recurs throughout the work). The chapter offers a critical reflection on minstrel songs, orientalism, and racist cultural appropriation.[16] For example, one hour is given over to a performance of the *Mikado* set on Mars to contest or defamiliarise its cultural and racial appropriations.

---

[15] http://www.smh.com.au/nsw/vandals-deface-hyde-park-statues-in-australia-day-protest-20170825-gy4pc3.html;
http://www.theage.com.au/victoria/historic-statues-where-women-and-indigenous-people-go-missing-20170831-gy8ev2.html
[16] https://www.theguardian.com/stage/2017/sep/13/taylor-mac-on-queering-history-someone-like-me-doesnt-normally-get-to-represent-america

These critiques of racist appropriations and stereotypes are offered in the show as part of a broader critical reflection on 'cheap sentiment'. Through reference to songs like 'After the Ball', Mac expands on how people have often cultivated a culture of 'cheap sentiment' to cope with the injuries inflicted on others in an unjust society, and to feel better about bad situations. Problematic stereotypes, exclusionary histories, depoliticized texts and formulaic character narratives can characterize cheap sentiment – it serves specific arrangements of power: 'When you're trying to validate a system, what is needed is cheap sentiment.'[17]

This is a frank assessment, presented starkly with the house lights all up bright near the end of the chapter. It is a historical observation delivered with resonance for today's times. How might we observe cheap sentiment circulating in culture today? Later, Mac tells a story about Nina Simone's 'Mississippi Goddamn', and about how one day Mac heard the song being played in a supermarket – but with all the lyrics removed, so that it was suitable background music to encourage the convivial consumption of the supermarket shopper. In protest against the cheap sentiment of stripping the politics – and Simone's voice – from the song, Mac sings the song with Simone's lyrics restored, but only after asking all of us to promise that after the show we would go home and watch Simone sing it online. In Mac's version, Simone's lyrics are slightly modified for the Australian context: 'everybody knows about Mississippi' but 'everybody knows about Manus' as well. Even though this chapter's focus is historical, Mac continually appears to ask questions of the present, and against cheap sentiment Mac draws on a wide range of cultural sources. For example, in one especially compelling section of the show, Mac recites some work by Walt Whitman which makes the audience ecstatic. This use of Whitman's democratic vision is only one example of how this show inventively draws on the past to inspire hope for the future.

---

[17] http://hudsonreview.com/2017/01/the-brooklyn-marathon-taylor-macs-a-24-decade-history-of-popular-music/#.Wfv0pK10ii4

Dreaming the Culture Forward

As a 'radical faerie realness ritual sacrifice,'[18] the elaborately conceived and structured show contains many ritualized components. A performer leaves the stage each hour, until we are left with only Mac for the final hour; some refrains are repeated across the work ('honour the verb not the noun', or words to that effect); and each hour is punctuated by a costume change, with the costume gradually getting pulled apart (or sometimes put together) over the course of the hour/decade. The dancing, music, singing, activities and speaking all blend together like a fevered calling up of history's ghosts, a ritual for the future. Mac talks about how 'dreaming the culture forward' involves revisiting history, and making room for the stories of others; it involves 'honouring' the past, and the present. Mac says you 'dream the culture forward' by making things, by bringing together the separate things we all can bring, and by sharing them with each other. Soup is offered as a metaphor, and then literally offered, as we are asked to play characters from the Depression, waiting on a soup line: A meal of sustenance from the scraps available. Scraps, fragments, crumbs, rubble: life built amidst what remains. I think mine was pumpkin with coconut.

Things to do with Brokenness

Late in Chapter Three, Mac and the band perform a chilling version of the Johnny Cash song, 'Ghost riders in the sky'[19], as the show confronts the horror of the American bombings of Japan at the end of World War Two. Reciting Auden's 'A Walk in the Dark',[20] Mac invites us to reflect on the question: How can one live with such a terrifying history? Death, weight and history resurface throughout the final hours of the show. To

---

[18] http://sometimesmelbourne.blogspot.com.au/2017/10/

[19] http://www.smh.com.au/entertainment/stage/melbourne-stage/almost-a-religious-experience-taylor-mac-opus-leaves-audience-weeping-for-more-20171021-gz5k07.html

[20] https://www.poeticous.com/w-h-auden/a-walk-after-dark; https://www.huffingtonpost.com/michael-giltz/theater-second-honeymoon_b_6518986.html

mark the Stonewall riots, Mac asks us to play pallbearers in a re-enactment of Judy Garland's funeral, carrying the body of a 'dead Judy Garland' (another audience member) through the audience and out of the theatre as the singer performs 'Goodbye Yellow Brick Road', that anthem of leaving the farm. In the 1986-1996 decade, a section of the show that explicitly focuses on AIDS, Mac's costume appears to be an embodied meditation on the notion of history, weight and death. Part of Mac's outfit involves what appears to be an oversized headpiece made up of screaming skulls, streaming what look like glittery tears.[21] History in glitter and skulls. It looks heavier than what I guess it is; I was surprised it didn't make Mac lose balance. The weight of all that history.

Metaphors play an important role in the show and Mac describes how the show was conceived in part as a metaphorical expression of Mac's teenage experience of the San Francisco AIDS walk. It was here, Mac first saw a homosexual person, 'and lots of them at once' (or words to that effect).[22] Mac describes the show as a way of recreating that intense experience of being exposed to queerness and queer history that Mac had not been taught in school. As Mac sings 'Blood Make Noise', history itself becomes audible.[23] Mac describes the show as a work of 'dandy revenge', and in the context of a knowable queer history so often marred by brutality, punishment and suffering, Mac deploys metaphors of carrying that history as a physical embodiment of survival, resistance, pleasure and transformation.

Lie Down or Get Up and Play

A striking moment during the show is when Mac asks the white people in the audience to perform their grief over the violence of racism, colonialism, and dispossession. Prior to this, Mac had moved the

---

[21] https://www.theguardian.com/stage/2017/oct/22/taylor-mac-review-24-decade-history-of-popular-music-melbourne-festival

[22] https://sfcurran.com/the-currant/interviews/taylor-made/

[23] https://ww2.kqed.org/arts/2016/10/12/how-i-survived-taylor-macs-24-hour-long-musical-history-lesson/

audience around, displacing the white people from the seats up front and centre and moving them to the sides, and inviting people of colour to come and take those seats. (There were lots of empty seats left over). Because there were not enough seats for the white people on the edges or margins, they all bunched up. Mac then asked the white people to look at the people of colour who had taken these seats and to make apology for all the racialized violence of colonialisms, to express grief, but to do it in a really exaggerated way. This was, as Mac, explained to give the people of colour an opportunity to see white people looking ridiculous, if nothing else. Through exaggeration, you can sometimes see the heart of the thing. This exaggeration of lament brought comedy, but also took us directly to that place of thinking beyond the grieving: after gestures of sorrow, what now? At one point Mac asks us to think about how all of this going on in the theatre is going to connect to what is happening outside, to the protests and struggles for change. How are we going to lift our brokenness into action? In the final moments of the show, with only Mac left on stage, 'Judy' gets the audience to join in the final chant: will you 'Lie down or get up and play?'[24], which we sing over and over. In the dark, it is like all of the ghosts that have been called up are asking the question of us, of what we will do with our time. Will you 'Lie down or get up and play?' 'I'm going to leave, but you'll keep singing', says Mac, or words that effect, and then 'Judy' is gone.

At the 'In Conversation' event following the show, Mac and the assembled company discussed the show's project of seeking to 'build bonds of community from exhaustion', out of the debris of having been 'torn apart' (or words similar). Mac describes how it is through the length of the show, the exhaustion, that people can come to take leave of themselves, and 'stretch towards' difference.

By the time of Mac's last performance, the closing of the Melbourne Festival, Mum was out of hospital and well enough to come along. After her being so ill it was such a celebration to be out. We got to the

[24] http://www.smh.com.au/entertainment/stage/melbourne-stage/almost-a-religious-experience-taylor-mac-opus-leaves-audience-weeping-for-more-20171021-gz5k07.html

theatre early because I knew the performance was general admission with no seating, so we would have to get close to the stage or else Mum would not be able to see much from her wheelchair.

On our way to the theatre we had passed people who had been out in Melbourne earlier that day demonstrating for a 'yes' vote and for marriage equality; some were heading home and some were coming to the show. Tonight, Mac said, is all about 'just singing the gay songs'; there was a feeling of celebration and solidarity in the air: 'Born to Run', 'Gimme Shelter', and 'Purple Rain': 'Honey … I know times are changing/It's time we all reach out for something new, that means the 'no' voters too'.[25] As an encore, Mac led the audience in a joyful version of 'Xanadu', a song that hadn't appeared in the *24 Decade* show, and offered as a queer prayer for Olivia Newton-John on news of her cancer returning. Then Mac crowd-surfed out of the show, heading to a late flight to Myanmar, while Machine Dazzle threw handfuls of glitter confetti into the audience, and the crew threw purple Lesbian Avenger-replica balloons ('Ask about lesbian lives'). During the show, Mac had thrown parts of the costume into the audience and we went home with Mum draped in a fragment from Mac's dress – a purple fabric that somehow seemed to shed glitter, leaving a trail in the wake of Mum's chair.

Looking back, October was a strange month, a month of raising ghosts of many kinds, of living with some, while leaving others behind. Outside the theatre, the survey mess was carrying on, but inside it wasn't setting the terms of what was going on. While the survey was a big part of October this was not a piece about that October experience because I don't want the survey to take over everything, to take over the times and how we recall them. I have not wanted that time to take over this time. And Mac's show demonstrates how you can do things differently, with the time you have. As Queer History Month comes

---

[25] 'Purple Rain', by Prince & The Revolution, adapted and performed by Taylor Mac and band.

around next year, I wonder how this year's ghosts will be remembered, and which ones we might forget?

––––––––––––––––

Daniel Marshall PhD is a Senior Lecturer in Literature in the School of Communication and Creative Arts, and convener of the Gender and Sexuality Studies Major, at Deakin University, Melbourne. Daniel has held positions as a Research Fellow at ARCSHS (La Trobe), an invited Visiting Scholar at the Center for LGBTQ Studies (New York) and at the Weeks Centre for Social and Policy Research (London). A past president of the Australian Lesbian and Gay Archives, he helped launch Australia's first LGBTI+ History Month in 2016.

Daniel thanks Valda Marshall and Duane Duncan for their feedback on this piece.

Still Dreaming | GUY JAMES WHITWORTH

I want

CHRISTOPHER BRYANT

FROM *INTOXICATION*

I want your arms.

I want your smile.

I want your talent.

I want to trust you, wholly, despite my misgivings.

I want to be honest. Really honest: as honest as you deserve.

I want that thing where you walk into a room and everyone just goes nuts over you, like, really loses it with joy, like: 'You're here, woo, hooray!'

I want to be sober.

I want you to get off *Grindr*.

I want you to read my work. Like, *really* read it, beginning to end, even the stuff that nobody else has read, and, gonna be honest: I want you to love it.

I want to be happy. I don't really know what that means, not really, but I want it just the same. Like, not in the melodramatic, 'I don't know what being happy means so I'm gonna slit my wrists to *My Chemical Romance*' teenaged emo kind of way, just in the way where I don't think I actually comprehend happiness, genuinely and conceptually.

I want you to send me those pictures again. You know … the ones you took of you in the mirror hard and jerking off. My phone died – well, actually, it committed suicide, fell headlong into the toilet just as I flushed it, and anyway, it's water-damaged, but I'd really like to still have a copy of them, they make me feel… alive.

I want to do everything to you.

I want you to do everything to me.

I want you to do everything *with* me.

I want to navigate the fine line between being the kind of fun and sassy honest person who takes no shit and speaks his feelings, and being the kind of person who just vomits unmitigated emotion over someone he's just met and cries in supermarkets.

I want to know what I'm doing.

Christopher Bryant is a Griffin Award nominated playwright, performer, and NIDA graduate. Recent work includes his 'talented and thoughtful' play *Intoxication,* which has toured the country in 2017 after winning the Queer Development Award in the Melbourne Fringe. He's been published by Play Lab, Australian Plays, and Hello Mr. Magazine, and teaches with Monash University, where he's currently completing his Ph.D.

Greetings from New York

MICHAEL BERNARD KELLY

MANHATTAN, SEPTEMBER 2017

Dear Family and Friends,

I am writing to you on a sunny autumn afternoon in New York
State, and sending you love and warm greetings.

It is now a bit more than three months since I set off from
Tullamarine airport for Manhattan, and it seems high time that I wrote
and let you know that I am thinking of you, as well as sharing with you
some of my experiences. Please excuse this group email – I am not a
fan of the genre, but at least it allows me to reach out and say hello to
you.

It has been a very rich time on many levels – but not without its
challenges and demands. Still, every time I was tempted to complain
about the intensely hot and humid summer in Manhattan, I reminded
myself that missing Melbourne's winter was not a bad trade-off – some
nights in July, for example, could be 26C with 80% humidity!

The month-long Research Colloquium, which I participated in in
July, was a great experience, and one moment stands out. As part of the
program, we each took at least an hour to share something of the
overall project we are involved in, and then invite discussion,
questioning and ideas. When we had gone all around the circle – which

was about half way through the month – I sat back and let myself be amazed by the many diverse ways in which these twelve people were working for transformation in our world.

That week I had the chance to have a discussion, in some depth, with Dr Christian Scharen, one of the key people who organised the Colloquium, and I asked him how these specific individuals were selected from the fifty or so who applied. He said that a key factor was that the scholars had to be more than just academics – they had to be people who were actively engaged, in some radical way, in bringing about change.

So, we had Francisco, a fiery young Lutheran leader who is studying a once all-white Lutheran congregation in New York that had transitioned peacefully and organically to being mainly a black community – and this would become part of his challenge to the whole Lutheran church in the USA. We had Amber, a dynamic young academic from St Louis, who is trans and a person of colour, and who is writing a book-length 'Letter to my Gender-fluid child'. We had Mark, a professor from Tennessee who is seeking to re-invigorate the Protestant left in the USA, and revitalise its commitment to social justice. We had Ann, a university lecturer and poet from York in the UK, who is seeking to develop a 'wild, Gaia-like sensibility as a way of rethinking our current world problems' in social, political, personal and environmental areas, and who is passionate about 'staying with the trouble' as a strategy of hope. We had Kate, a theologian from Cincinnati who does radical work with prisoners who are transitioning back into the community, and who is passionate about developing theological and prophetic approaches to 'the new racial caste system that is mass incarceration and which decimates families and communities materially and emotionally'. We had Zaynab, a Muslim woman of colour who is studying the roots of the exclusion/regulation of women in traditional Muslim and Jewish ritual spaces, and seeking to find new ways to reform ancient practices. We had Ursula, a Lutheran pastor and theologian from Germany, who is studying and writing about the church's attempts, and failures, in dealing with Luther's anti-semitic writings, and seeking to explore new frontiers in Jewish-

Lutheran relations. We had Lek, a young Buddhist monk from Thailand, who was formerly a lawyer and an environmental activist, and who is now committed to developing a radical new approach to social justice within the whole Theravadan Buddhist tradition. We had Aimee from New York, who is studying how governments, local councils and real estate developers have used racially based policies to change whole neighbourhoods, to distort patterns of home ownership, and to accumulate wealth by systematically disenfranchising black communities. We had Sharon, from York in the UK, who is studying the emergence of women priests in the Anglican church in the UK, and exploring the ways they have become co-opted by the power structure, or, by contrast, have become resistors and reformers. And then of course, there was this fellow from Australia …

As I looked around that circle, I was moved to tears by the many different stories, by the differing passions and pathways, and by the common commitment to do what we could, in our own corner of this troubled world, to nurture more hope, more light, more justice, more compassion – and new kinds of vision. As I write these words, I am also deeply aware of you, dear friends, and the many different ways each of us tries to nurture a future that is more hopeful, more loving and more just.

When the Colloquium ended I was invited to spend August at a small retreat centre about ninety minutes north of Manhattan – it is run by a gay couple who are old friends of mine from my time in California in the early 1990s. It was lovely to spend some time in the country after the buzz of the city, and to settle into a gentler pace …

Throughout September I was back in the city, apartment-sitting for some friends, and catching up with some new contacts and colleagues. One the gifts of New York is that it brings all kinds of people together. One of the new friends I have made this time around, for example, has been Fr Bryan Massingale, who is a professor of moral theology at Fordham University – a Jesuit college in the city. He is the foremost theologian specialising in issues of racism and the Catholic Church. Getting to know him has been a highlight of my time here, and his interest in my own writing has been a real gift and a great affirmation.

Knowing him has also made events like those in Charlottesville feel much closer and more urgent. Bryan was deeply disturbed and angered not only by the marches, the torches, and the racist and anti-semitic chants – he was, in some ways, even more distressed by the lukewarm responses from so many Catholic bishops. This is a dangerous and uncertain time in the US, and it is an honour to know someone like Bryan.

On Friday night last I took the train from Grand Central Station – on an unseasonably warm night, and headed back to the retreat centre – where autumn is finally beginning to colour the leaves. It's good to be back in the quiet – and I need to get to some serious writing if I am ever to deliver on my book deal with Routledge! My time in the city was great, though, with many meetings with friends, lots of meals, and a range of theatrical experiences – from the sublime to the (almost) ridiculous. As you can imagine, I have to manage my health and my energy very carefully when I am travelling and staying in one apartment after another, and New York City is both irresistible and exhausting.

I keep up-to-date fairly well with news from home – and it seems lots of people are working hard and with great passion to bring about marriage equality. It is especially great to see Fr Frank Brennan, the two major Jesuit schools, and countless Christians from all denominations speaking up for LGBT people, and for our relationships. Just a few years back, when I was deeply involved in the Rainbow Sash Movement, voices and views like these would have been unimaginable. Hopefully Martin Luther King was right, and the arc of history does bend towards justice …

Being here in the US, though, as this time is unsettling and disturbing. More than once a New Yorker has expressed real concern about the possibility of the city becoming a target in a North Korean conflict – and everyone who is sane continues to be horrified by the dangerous antics of Donald Trump, who is really exposing the deep darkness that has always been there in the soul of America. As Fr Massingale puts it, 'Trump is an exaggeration – but he is not an aberration'. This is undoubtedly the most unsettled and disturbing time

I have ever experienced in the US – and I have coming here for extended periods since 1989.

For all that, however, there is so much about this country, and especially about New York, that is extraordinary and wonderful – for example, I attended a recent open debate/discussion on LGBT issues and the Catholic Church at Fordham University here in New York. A well-known Jesuit, Fr James Martin, has written a book about 'building bridges' between the LGBTI community and the hierarchy of the church – basing it on the teachings about sensitivity, compassion and respect. It's important work, but it does skirt the deeper issues. He was challenged by the man who is Chair of the Theology Department at Fordham, who is openly gay and married to his partner. This is the kind of event that New York offers ...

I must admit that it is reassuring to have a ready passage back to Australia, even with all of our own craziness and darkness. Speaking of which, my current plan is to head across to the west coast, probably San Francisco, in early December, and then fly back home, arriving on December 14. I am sure I will be very ready to be home.

For now, though, I will enjoy the changing of the leaves and the brilliant autumn colours and the cool crisp days – just as I hope you are enjoying the coming of springtime. Please know that, despite the distances, you are in my thoughts and prayers each day, and I look forward very much to our next coffee, meal or glass of wine – preferably somewhere by the beach!

———————————

Michael Bernard Kelly PhD is an Adjunct Research Associate with the Centre for Religious Studies at Monash University. He is the author of *Seduced by Grace: Contemporary Spirituality, Gay Experience and Christian Faith* and the video lecture series *The Erotic Contemplative*.

Making News in 2017

STAR OBSERVER

January

Aboriginal LGBTI community to lead Melbourne's pride march for the first time
Imam calls for more multicultural and religious voices in LGBTI community
Massive drop in new HIV cases in Brisbane
Government provides funding for Australia's lesbian and gay archives
Judge calls for overhaul of 'inhumane' court process for trans teens

February

Liberal MPs to push for free vote on same-sex marriage
Public schools in NSW banned from teaching gender theory
Michelle Heyman nominated for LGBTI sports personality of the year award
Northern Territory stars set to shine at Mardi Gras
Moonlight becomes first LGBT film to win Oscar for Best Picture
Research finds LGBTI Australians have served in military since World War II

March

Italy recognises both gay dads of surrogate babies
Community welcomes Coopers' decision to back marriage equality
Majority of voters in 12 of the most conservative seats back marriage equality
Same-sex marriage postal vote 'sneaky', advocates say
Queensland scraps 'gay panic' defence
Melbourne cabaret to showcase queer performers of colour

April

AIDS Garden of Reflection opens in Canberra
New trans health service opens in Brisbane
Tasmania and New South Wales to dump Safe Schools
Rainbow wreath laid for LGBTI soldiers on ANZAC Day
Group supporting older gay and bi men in Victoria risks closure

May

Melbourne exhibition to showcase trans artists
Qantas CEO Alan Joyce attacked with pie over marriage equality
Volunteers championed in Melbourne's LGBTI community
HIV-positive lifespan now close to average
Bake sale in Brisbane raises funds to support queer men in Chechnya
Beirut holds Arab world's first ever pride festival

June

Aussie horror monster becomes unlikely queer icon
Brisbane rainbow artwork to be restored after vandalism
Calls to end forced divorce for trans partners in Australia
More same-sex couples in Australia than ever before: census
Minister for Health launches plan to eliminate HIV in Victoria

July

Gay orgy at Cardinal's apartment raided by Vatican police
Aussie report highlights queer women's health needs
Malta latest country to legalise same-sex marriage before Australia
Indonesia attempts to hide gay floggings
Celebs help draw attention to gay Chechnya crisis
Freddie Mercury biopic to omit AIDS crisis
The Bachelor has a bisexual contestant and the internet can't handle it

August

Large group of bisexual dolphins off WA coast
Plebiscite bill fails Senate with $122 million postal vote likely
Aussie singer's song chosen as official anthem of Hamburg Pride
Pakistan to outlaw anti-trans discrimination
Gay farmer named Young Farmer of the Year
Activists pepper-sprayed by skinheads at St Petersburg Pride
Sydney drag queens rescue man from homophobic attack
Gay dating app cops backlash for banning HIV-positive guys

September

Canberra's marriage equality rally largest in city's history
L'Oréal fires trans model for slamming white supremacy
Queer counselling service sees 25 per cent spike in calls
Gay dads open up about fostering their three gorgeous children
Brisbane's gay rugby team wins Purchas Cup
Tasmania to wipe gay and trans criminal records
Roughly 20 people turned up to the 'straight lives matter' rally
Macklemore will sing his marriage equality anthem at the NRL Grand Final

October

Fred Nile is worried gays will create a new country with 'Same Love' as their
national anthem
More than 50 people arrested in Egypt anti-LGBTI crackdown
Tireless HIV activist Levinia Crooks passes away
Shepparton festival celebrates LGBTI pride
Aboriginal elder urges Australians to vote Yes
On Intersex Awareness Day advocates call for an end to forced surgery

November

Drag in the desert: Broken Heel takes us back to the birthplace of Priscilla
Trans footballer says she doesn't agree with AFL's decision to ban her
Homeless trans people denied rentals in Victoria
Kenyan official blames tourists for gay lions
Latest poll predicts huge Yes victory for marriage equality
LGBTI community to call for safety of men imprisoned on Manus
Activists Peter and Bon to be honoured with lifetime achievement award
Rabbi compares gay people to 'space aliens'
Rainbows fly high as Australia votes Yes to marriage equality
Drag star Violet Chachki is the face of new lingerie line
Rural and regional areas in Australia are becoming more LGBTI accepting
Perth teacher fired after coming out as gay

December

Bent Street – new LGBTIQA+ magazine of art, writing and ideas first issue

The Year in Queer 2017

JESS JONES

This has been an eventful year, with no end of news affecting the LGBTI community, both locally and internationally. *Star Observer* has covered all the important queer news in 2017. We have shared breaking news with Australia, as well as interviewing people in the LGBTI community, celebrities and politicians to bring readers their stories.

In Australia, this year's major news has been the marriage equality debate. As the anti-LGBTI Coalition for Marriage launched a bizarre series of ads that failed to address the matter of marriage, focusing instead on demonising LGBTI young people, the $122 million postal survey arguably became a de facto vote on whether being queer or trans is acceptable. Both sides of the debate have had some unlikely allies, with over 100 Australian religious leaders speaking out in support of marriage equality, while a few gay people including Milo Yiannopoulos publicly said they are against it.

Homophobia and transphobia stirred up by the marriage equality debate led to attacks around Australia, with properties displaying rainbow flags targeted by vandals, swastikas and anti-gay slogans appearing in public spaces, and at least two alleged assaults of young trans people.

Polls throughout the survey period nonetheless showed high support for marriage equality, making a Yes outcome seem likely. Prime

Minister Malcolm Turnbull suggested same-sex marriages could be a reality before the end of the year in the event of a Yes win. In March, intersex activists from around Australia and New Zealand met in Sydney to launch the Darlington Statement, which issues key priorities for the intersex community. Chief among these priorities was bodily autonomy and an end to forced surgeries for babies and children born with intersex variations.

Other countries are already moving to outlaw such unnecessary surgeries, including Portugal, which announced in May it would ban them. This is in line with a new Amnesty International report that condemns so-called 'normalising' surgeries on intersex babies.

Much-loved LGBTI rights activist Peter 'Bon' Bonsall-Boone passed away in May. He was survived by his partner of 50 years, Peter de Waal, with whom he had campaigned for marriage equality prior to his death. Bon was posthumously awarded an Order of Australia for his tireless advocacy work.

This year marks the 20th anniversary of Ellen DeGeneres coming out, leading to her show *Ellen* being cancelled at the time. She opened up about the controversy that coming out caused in the 90s, saying she even received death threats.

Plenty more celebrities came out this year, including Barry Manilow announcing he is gay, K-pop star Hansol coming out as asexual, and Aaron Carter revealing he is bisexual.

In the US, President Donald Trump decreed by tweet in July that trans people would be banned from the military. In the immediate wake of the announcement, calls to suicide hotlines by trans people in the US doubled. In November, a federal court overruled the ban, deeming it to have been rooted in transphobia and unconstitutional. Conservative commentator Mark Latham was inspired by Trump's tweet to suggest that Australia should follow suit in banning trans people from the Defence Force. After One Nation senator Pauline Hanson raised concerns about the cost of military healthcare for trans people, the Defence Force stated that such expenses are a vanishingly small part of the Defence Force's medical budget, dismissing the matter as 'hysterical'.

News of a gay persecution crisis in the Russian region of Chechnya has slowly emerged over the year. Reports began emerging in April of concentration camps where gay and bi men have been detained, tortured and killed. Chechen officials denied the camps exist, claiming there are no gays in the republic. Numerous international reports and interviews with victims have now been corroborated by Human Rights Watch, in what has been called a genocide.

In the latter half of the year, authorities in Azerbaijan reportedly began a similar crackdown on the LGBTI community, arresting and torturing gay and trans people. Police denied that the arrests were related to gender or sexuality, alleging that they were connected to prostitution offences.

In Indonesia, authorities in the conservative province of Aceh have caned hundreds of people for crimes including homosexuality. Over 100 men were also arrested at a gay sauna in the capital of Jakarta. In positive international news, marriage equality was legalised in Malta, Finland and Germany this year, with Taiwan also passing legislation that will allow same-sex marriage. Around the world, 25 countries have now passed laws granting marriage equality.

Several beauty brands around the world featured trans models in their campaigns for the first time. One of the most high-profile was Munroe Bergdorf, who was controversially let go by L'Oréal UK after using her platform to speak out against racism. Ines Rau became the first trans woman to be featured as a centrefold in *Playboy*, dividing readers and inciting controversy on social media.

On November 15 the result of the marriage equality postal survey was announced. With over 12 million people having had their say, the result was an ovewhelming 61.6 per cent Yes. Every state and territory returned a majority Yes vote.

In a very eventful year of queer news, a consistent theme has been that some of the invisible letters in LGBTI+ are becoming more recognised. Issues affecting trans, bisexual, intersex and asexual people are starting to gain more visibility, and this progress will hopefully continue. We're looking forward to continuing to bring you the important news as it does.

Star Observer is Australia's longest running and most respected LGBTI media outlet, with a news website and national monthly magazine. It has been proudly and independently covering LGBTI news since 1979. http://starobserver.com.au.

Jess Jones is *Star Observer*'s senior journalist, based in Brisbane. With a background that includes public health and technical writing, his many interests include gender, health and travel. https://www.facebook.com/JessJonesAU

The Long Road Home

RODNEY CROOME

How marriage equality will unlock a better future for Australia

You would think after a two month postal survey there is nothing left to say about marriage equality. But in my view we haven't even begun to talk about what it will really mean for Australia to allow same-sex couples to marry. The imperative of winning a popular vote meant the national Yes campaign avoided challenging old prejudices or triggering controversy of any kind. In the face of dire predictions from the No camp about the end of civilisation as we know it, the Yes campaign made marriage equality the smallest possible target, asserting that nothing will change except that same-sex couples will be able to marry. I was never comfortable with this approach and now I feel free to say why.

The grain of truth at the centre of the No campaign's many myths and distortions is that marriage equality will profoundly transform Australia. But that transformation will be for the better. The marriage equality debate is thirteen years old, and has been shaped by successive governments, most major national institutions and the contributions of millions of Australians who support and oppose the reform. As a result, marriage equality has acquired a meaning greater than itself.

It is no longer just about allowing same-sex couples to walk down the aisle, as important as that is. It has become the stage upon which the nation is playing out all its tensions, frustrations and divisions. It has become a metaphor for an Australia that is more open to the world, more inclusive of those who are different and more equal in the opportunities it allows its citizens.

———————

Allowing same-sex couples to marry will confirm once and for all that marriage is now something very different, more democratic and much better.

———————

Future generations will look back on the current postal survey in the same way we look back on the referendum on Indigenous rights in 1967. Although the question was a narrow one about whether Aborigines should be counted in the Census, we think of it as a pivot upon which Australian history swung. The achievement of marriage equality will be the same. Let me give you some concrete examples of what I believe will be the wider ramifications of marriage equality.

MARRIAGE

Marriage equality will renovate and restore the institution of marriage. Since the twentieth century battles over contraception, no fault divorce, rape in marriage, and rights for de facto couples, marriage has been a cultural battle field. Some people want to return marriage to a mythical time when, according to God's ordinance, husbands and fathers ruled over their households, married women put their families before their own fulfilment, and divorce was unacceptable because marriage wasn't about love, it was about respectability, property and procreation. Allowing same-sex couples to marry will confirm once and for all that marriage is now something very different, more democratic and much better. It will be the union of two people who are equals, who freely of their own volition choose if, when and how to marry, who define for themselves what their marriage means, and who publicly commit to each other for no greater reason, because there is no greater reason, than they love one another. Like most Australians, especially younger ones, I believe love, commitment and willing self-sacrifice are what make a marriage. I believe what I have with my partner is more a marriage than the compulsory, loveless, sexist, cultural straightjacket No campaigners call marriage. Marriage equality will finally and conclusively confirm this, thereby giving the institution a renewed lease of life and greater relevance to coming generations.

HUMAN RIGHTS

Another very specific impact of marriage equality will be to give the movement for a charter of human rights greater urgency and purchase. Australia's lateness to marriage equality is due in large part to the fact we are the only western country without national protections for human rights including the right to equality. Such protections have been crucial to achieving marriage equality from Canada and the US, through Mexico and Brasil, to South Africa and Taiwan. Adding to the argument for a human rights charter is Parliament's decision to abdicate its responsibility by having a public vote on marriage equality.

The postal survey is an admission by Parliament that it's not up to the job of making hard decisions about intractable human rights issues, that it isn't supreme and that a superior adjudicator is sometimes required. Obviously, the postal survey with its many flaws is not the answer to Parliament's self-confessed failure. That answer is a charter of human rights that gives courts the power to rule on human rights abuses. The postal survey also highlights the need for human rights protections in another, quite unexpected way.

The No case has lost the argument against same-sex couples marrying so it has tried to stir up fears about marriage equality infringing freedom of religion and freedom of speech, even though this is no evidence of this from overseas. The shard of truth in this otherwise baseless fear campaign is that freedom and religion and speech are not properly protected in Australia. As the recent High

Court decision against Tasmania's draconian protest laws reminded us, free speech is at best 'implied' in the Constitution. The No campaign has failed to mount an effective case against marriage equality, but it has run a strong case for a national charter of rights.

GOVERNING AUSTRALIA

Now let's turn to the way Australia is governed and what influence we as ordinary citizens have over it. Successive Australian prime ministers have failed miserably in dealing with marriage equality. They have been wildly out of touch with popular opinion, they have shown no leadership, they have been in hock to the minority religious and authoritarian caucuses in their respective parties. Again, this contrasts with those countries that have achieved marriage equality through legislation where leadership by heads of government, on the left and right, has been critical.

Achieving marriage equality will improve how we are governed in several ways. The campaign has already exposed how out of touch our politicians are, and how self-referential they have become. Our national Parliament is the Palace of Versailles without the fancy chandeliers. In response, millions of Australians have chosen to engage with the marriage equality campaign, through letter writing, lobbying, marching and finally voting.

We did this in order to prod our politicians into action. Our collective message is, if you won't do what's right, we will force you to. When this grassroots, from-the-ground-up campaign, achieves its goal it will send the clearest signal possible that politicians cannot evade their responsibility to the community. Marriage equality will demonstrate to everyday Australians that positive change is possible and that we can be instrumental in creating that change. It will be a much-needed reminder that our destiny as a nation is in the hands of its people, not its politicians.

No less important, when we achieve marriage equality it will be because we have successfully challenged the disproportionate power of religious dogmatists and anti-democratic authoritarians in our political system. Here I'm talking about people who have concocted a life and death culture war out of marriage equality. In their eyes the idea that our gender doesn't determine our rights or identity is some kind of radical global left wing conspiracy against western civilisation. For them the postal survey is not the 1967 Aboriginal referendum but the 1951 referendum about banning the Communist Party.

Don't get me wrong, I believe a healthy democracy should represent all views. But those who have a sentimental attachment to an Australia that never was control the levers of power to a far greater extent than their support in the electorate warrants. Achieving marriage equality will expose their Henny Penny fear campaigns as just so much hot air. It will affirm that what lies in our heart is more important than what is between our legs. It will say the future is not something to run from. It will confirm that moral improvement and social progress are possible and desirable, not just on LGBTI issues but on every issue. It will be an antidote to the poisonous pessimism of our age.

THE LGBTI COMMUNITY

Given how long marriage equality has taken, few Australians have more reason for pessimism than LGBTI people. But my message is to take hope. Marriage equality promises a profound transformation in our lives. The very worst stereotypes of LGBTI people take refuge in the Marriage Act as it stands. When LGBTI people are explicitly excluded from an institution that defines love, commitment and family, the message is that we not only can never experience these things, but that we are somehow a threat to them. You cannot under-estimate the profound damage this causes, and in equal measure the healing that will come from marriage equality.

More than this, I believe marriage equality will help dig out the deeply-rooted historical weeds of fear, loathing and violence towards LGBTI people. In *The Fatal Shore*, Robert Hughes argued that the rhetoric of the nineteenth century movement against convict transportation – rhetoric that focused obsessively on the link between convictism and unnatural vice – infected Australian national identity with homophobia. I believe this to be true because of my experience in Tasmania where the struggles for gay equality and against the shadow of convictism have lasted longest, been most difficult, and have been linked by the same deep anxiety about losing our veneer of respectability. In Tasmania the cure for all these old fears, phobias and anxieties was the decriminalisation of homosexuality in 1997. That reform and the debate that led up to it did more than anything else to help our island come to terms with its anti-gay history and move on from hate. Marriage equality will do the same for the nation as a whole.

It is no longer just about equality or inclusion, as important as they are. It is also now about belonging. Belonging is a very radical idea.

After so many heartfelt personal conversations, so much support from community and business leaders, after so many rainbow flags hoisted high, how could Australia be anything but a much better place. My prediction is that, like Tasmania before it, the nation will quickly go from worst to best on LGBTI equality. The rubber band of public policy has been stretched so far in one direction, it will soon shoot all the way in the other. Marriage equality will be what releases it. As well as changing how LGBTI people are viewed by others, marriage equality will change how we see ourselves.

Over the last few years I have noticed a small but profound change in the way LGBTI people talk about marriage equality. It is no longer just about equality or inclusion, as important as they are. It is also now about belonging. Belonging is a very radical idea. While equality can be recognised and inclusion can be granted, belonging can only ever be negotiated between those who feel they own an identity and those who feel dispossessed of that identity. That negotiation is almost always difficult and painful, and it changes everyone involved in unpredictable ways, but if it succeeds we become truly, fully the people we were meant to be. Just as marriage equality is a metaphor for positive political and social change across the community, so it has become a metaphor in the eyes of many LGBTI people for our desire to truly belong in the families, faiths, communities of place and communities of interest that have shaped who we are. The cruel god called Prejudice has cast LGBTI people far from where we belong, and now, with marriage equality lighting our way, we are finally walking the long road home.

TURNING POWER INTO LOVE

In all the long years I have advocated for marriage equality I have shared the stage with many people who have talked about its benefits. But in all these millions or words, one sentence stands out. It was spoken, and you may not expect this, by an Anglican minister in Toowoomba. It says everything I have been trying to say this evening: When we have marriage equality, it will be one more healing release from clinging to privileges, one more letting go of prejudices, one more turning of power into love.

> But this noble idea, this turning of power into love, will only occur if marriage equality is true equality. Already, opponents of marriage equality are erecting the next hurdle to it.

As Australia votes Yes, they intend to punch holes in Australia's anti-discrimination laws that will allow married same-sex partners to be discriminated against, to be refused service by businesses, to be sacked from their jobs, to have their marital status ignored, to be openly vilified. Following their counterparts in the United States, Australia's radical right will seek to dignify their campaign to perpetuate discrimination by saying they are protecting religious freedom and freedom of speech. But what they are really about is maintaining privilege, their own legal privilege to judge the worthy from the unworthy. I have not given over a decade of my life to marriage equality to see it compromised in this way.

If surveys in the LGBTI community are anything to go by, LGBTI Australians overwhelmingly agree. We will resist any caveats and carve outs that perpetuate discrimination, even if that means we have to wait a little longer for the reform we hold dear. I'm heartened to see polls released just this week show an emphatic majority of Australians agree any amendment to the Marriage Act should treat all couples equally. If marriage equality is to transform our nation for the better, in the ways I have described tonight, be assured many Australians gay and straight will fight as hard as ever to ensure it is true marriage equality, and not some nasty travesty. Those who come after us deserve nothing less of us.

———————————

Rodney Croome AM wrote this contribution for his 2017 Sally Duncanson Memorial Lecture at the University of Tasmania, which he delivered in November 2017. Rodney Croome is a long-time advocate for the equal rights of LGBTI people. In particular he led the campaign to decriminalise homosexuality in Tasmania and has been at the forefront of the marriage equality debate. He has been honoured for his work by being named as a Member of the Order of Australia and Tasmanian Australian of the Year in 2015.

Bent Street is published by Clouds of Magellan Press, Melbourne

www.cloudsofmagellanpress.net